DESIGN AND COMMUNICATION

▸ FOR FOUNDATION COURSES ◂

DESIGN AND COMMUNICATION

▸ FOR FOUNDATION COURSES ◂

Peter Gowers

Blackie

DESIGN AND COMMUNICATION
▸ FOR FOUNDATION COURSES ◂

ISBN 0 216 92382 4
First published 1988

Illustrated by the Author
Cartoons by David Till and Mike Gordon

Published by Blackie and Son Ltd
Bishopbriggs, Glasgow G64 2NZ
7 Leicester Place, London WC2H 7BP

British Library Cataloguing in Publication data

Gowers, Peter
Design and communication for foundation courses.
1. Visual communication
I. Title
001.55′3
ISBN 0-216-92382-4

Filmset by Advanced Filmsetters (Glasgow) Ltd
Printed in Great Britain

Preface

Design and Communication is a very important part of Craft, Design and Technology (CDT). No matter what design problem you have to solve, you always need to communicate your ideas. You can communicate your ideas in a variety of ways, but unless you do it clearly your solution may not work well. Solutions to design problems may be either two-dimensional, such as signs and symbols, or they may be three-dimensional, such as pop-up cards and working prototype models.

You will use many of the techniques and materials that are included in this book in Art as well as in CDT. There is a very close link between Art and CDT; both use visual communication to develop two and three-dimensional solutions. In fact, in many of the subjects that you study at school, you are asked to communicate ideas visually in pictures or diagrams. You can therefore make use of Design and Communication in much of your school work.

In this book I have tried to solve a design problem. The problem was how to help *you* to develop your ability to communicate your ideas through drawing and modelling so that you can solve your own design problems. The book looks at drawing, rendering and modelling techniques, and the materials you can use for them. There are sections on using line, shape, form, texture, colour, making pop-ups, models and the presentation of work. Although the section on presentation is at the back of the book, it may be a good idea to read it first. The way you present all your work is very important and it can say a lot about you! Take pride in all you do.

Developing and communicating solutions to design problems is not always easy, but it should always be enjoyable. I hope that this book will help to make it even more enjoyable for you. Have fun!

► *Peter Gowers*

Acknowledgments

The Author and Publishers wish to thank the following for permission to reproduce copyright material.

p.3 Package Aid Limited (top right)
p.6 Sonia Halliday Photographs (top left); Ronald Sheridan Photographs (bottom left); Royal Library (top right)
p.7 British Telecom (bottom right)
p.10 Seiko Time (UK) Ltd.
p.14 Transworld Eye (top left); Institute of Geological Sciences (middle left); Lead Development Association (bottom left); Lloyd C.P. Yam (right); Frank W Lane Photographs (centre photo)
p.17 Landor Associates (Lynx); Design in Action; Roger Gowers Designs
p.18 Dorma
p.19 National Cavity Insulation Association (top left); Aerofilms (middle left); Institute of Geological Sciences (bottom left and top right); Vasari (middle right); Michelin Tyre Company (bottom right); Forestry Commission (bottom right)
p.21 Porsche Cars Great Britain Limited
p.22 D.C. Thomson & Co. Ltd. (cartoon strip)
p.31 Department of Environment, Crown Copyright Photograph
p.33 Aliza Auerbach
p.34 Hornsea Pottery Co. Ltd. (bottom left); ICI Plastics Division (bottom right)
p.39 Times Newspapers Limited
p.43 Slater Harrison & Co. Ltd. (Colourcard)
p.44 Frank W Lane Photographs (left); ICI Paints Division (top and middle right); British Home Stores (logo)
p.58 (top right) The Lakes School, Windermere
p.62 Britain/Israel Public Affairs Committee
p.66 Rowntree Mackintosh Group (bottom right)
p.67 Lego UK Ltd.
p.77 Package Aid Limited (top left)
p.78 Ford (Insert artwork: *The Observer*)

All other photographs are copyright of the Author.

The Author would like to thank colleagues at Edge Hill College of Higher Education for their support and encouragement, and also those students who have allowed him to use examples of their work.

Contents

What is design and communication?

▸ DESIGN

Design is about solving problems. We can see the results of it all around us, wherever we are in the man-made world. Everything that has ever been made by people has been designed to meet a certain need—to solve a certain problem. People have used their knowledge of materials and technology to design solutions to all kinds of problems. A simple paper clip is a solution to a design problem, so is the most complex computer; an easy-to-read airport sign is one, and so is a space shuttle.

What problem is solved by each of these designs?

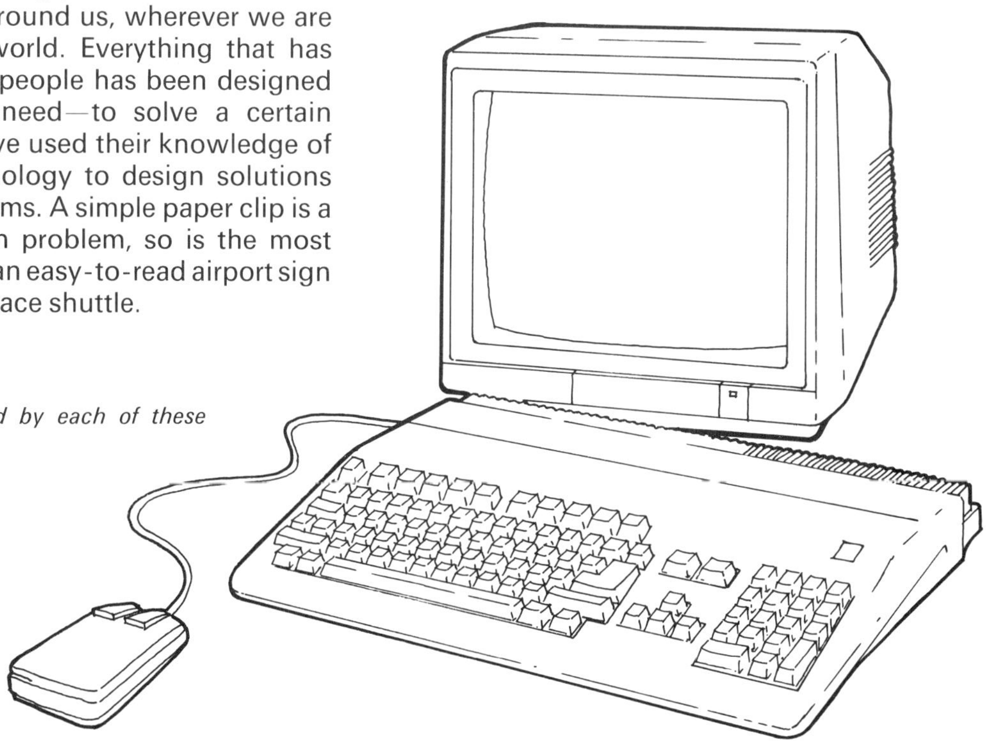

▸ COMMUNICATION

Communication is about the transfer of information. People can communicate using the five **senses** of sight, sound, touch, taste and smell. Sometimes we use only one sense by itself: reading a book or comic only involves sight. At other times, for example when watching television, we use a combination of senses. We receive a great deal of information through our eyes, however, and we live in a world in which our sense of sight is very important. Just close your eyes for a moment and think what life would be like if you could not see.

Writing is, of course, one of the most important means of communication which depends upon the use of our eyes. As the pace of modern life speeds up, however, drawings or **visual images** are gradually replacing written information in many places. Shapes, symbols and colours are used more and more to provide 'quick' information.

Old road signs consisted of words and phrases, but now, fewer signs have words on them. The signs used on our roads today are mostly symbols and they can be quickly and easily understood from a long distance away, or when you are travelling past them very quickly. Airport signs are another good example of the usefulness of symbols: simple symbols can be easily understood by people from all over the world, no matter what language they speak. The designer has developed a new **visual language** which can be understood at a glance.

The designer's visual language also includes the use of **models**. Models are often scaled-down (smaller than the real thing) three-dimensional objects which are built to test possible designs and for presentation.

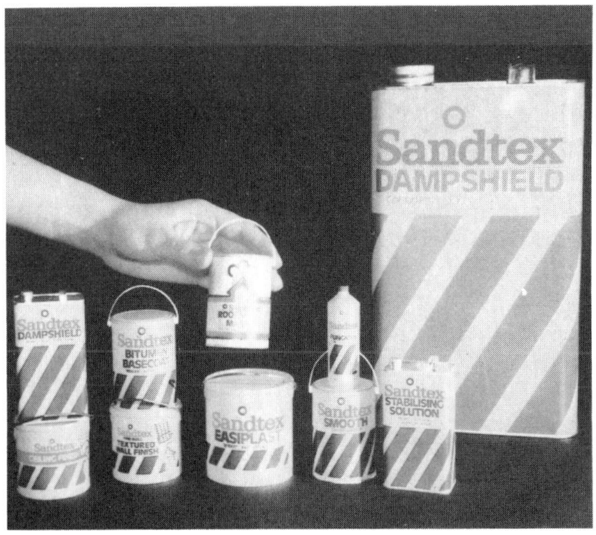

Scale models to present ideas for packaging

Design and communication, then, is about solving problems using a combination of words, drawings and models, and about communicating our solutions to other people. It is therefore very important that you learn to communicate your ideas clearly at all stages when you are developing your designs. This book will help you to do that.

Road signs must be quickly and easily understood

THE DESIGN CYCLE

The **design cycle** is used to develop solutions to a problem. The problem may seem quite simple or very complex, but if it is to be solved successfully, a logical method of working needs to be used. How and where do you start?

The first thing you must do is **identify the problem** and write a short statement about it. At first, your teacher may give you set problems to solve, but as you progress you should try to identify real problems for yourself which, if solved well, will be of benefit to you, your friends and others in the community.

Identify the problem

When you have been given or have identified the problem, you must write down exactly what is required. This statement is called the **brief**.

Write the brief

If you are to solve the brief successfully, you must gather as much helpful background information as possible. This can come from books, magazines, catalogues and from places like shops and museums. In other words, you must do some **research**.

Research and gather information

Record the information you have collected by cutting out pictures, and making notes and drawings in your sketchbook. In this way, you can build up your own store of information on design topics that interest you. Make sure you arrange your information in an ordered way so that you can easily find what you need.

Next, you must look at the brief very carefully and consider such things as size, materials, safety, colour and cost. From this, you can write a **specification**, which is a list of points you must remember when thinking about possible designs.

Look at possible materials for realization

Now you can use your research and specification to develop **ideas**. Your ideas should be put down in a logical way, using a combination of drawings and notes.

Sketch ideas

When you arrive at a possible solution, it may help to make a **mock-up** or **model**. Using this, you may be able to refine the design further by '**looping back**' to your drawings.

Make mock-ups

When you are happy with your solution, you can make more accurate **production drawings** so that you have the necessary information to make or **realize** the final design.

Realize the final design

Finally, you must **test** and **evaluate** the finished design to see how well it works. Does it answer the specification and solve the brief well? If not, you must ask yourself 'why?'. How could it be improved? Is a different sort of design needed? You can then 'loop back' again and make the necessary modifications to improve or change the design.

Test and evaluate the finished design

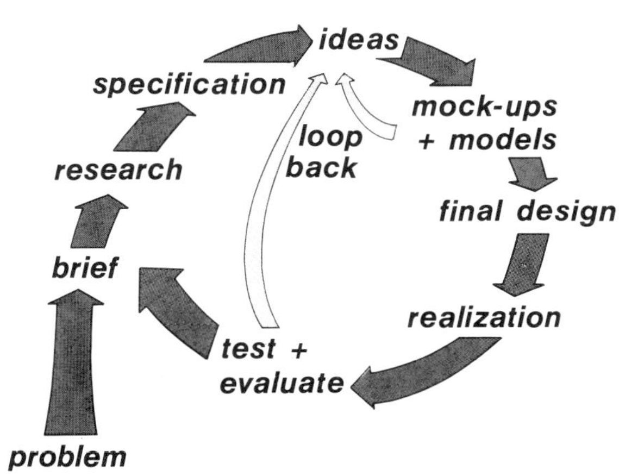

The design cycle

METHODS OF VISUAL COMMUNICATION

Communicating information through drawings is not new. From earliest times, people have used drawings and diagrams to illustrate their ideas and record events. Cavemen painted and drew on the walls of their caves.

The Egyptians used **hieroglyphics** as a picture alphabet. In some ways, the sorts of signs and symbols which are being used more and more in society today are rather like hieroglyphs.

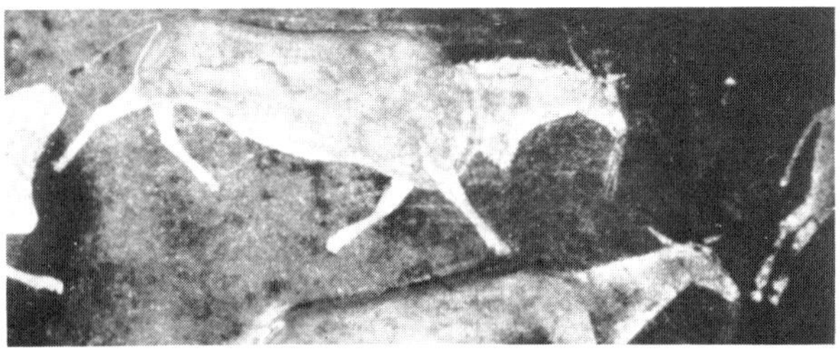

Cave paintings from Lascaux, France

Hieroglyphs from the ceiling of the tomb of Rameses VI

▶ NOTES AND DRAWINGS

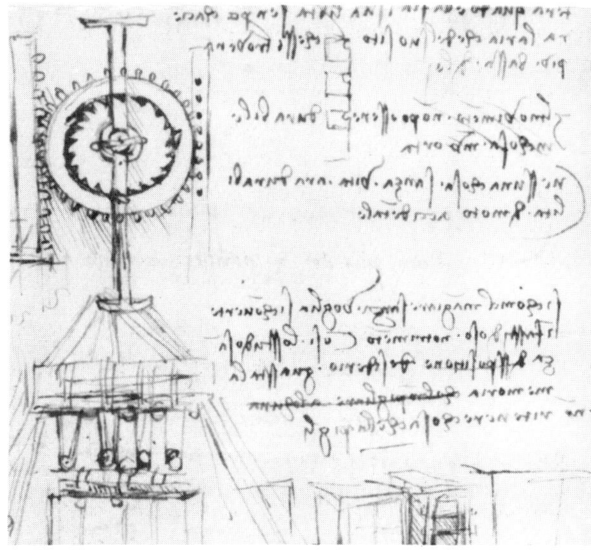

Some of Leonardo da Vinci's notes and drawings

Leonardo da Vinci (1452–1519) used notes and drawings to research and work out the ideas he developed from close observation of the world he lived in. At the time when he was working, da Vinci's ideas were so advanced that people thought he was a danger to society, so he had to write his notes back to front in order to continue working. You need to use a mirror to read them.

The present day designer also uses notes and drawings, and you can do the same to work out solutions to your own design assignments.

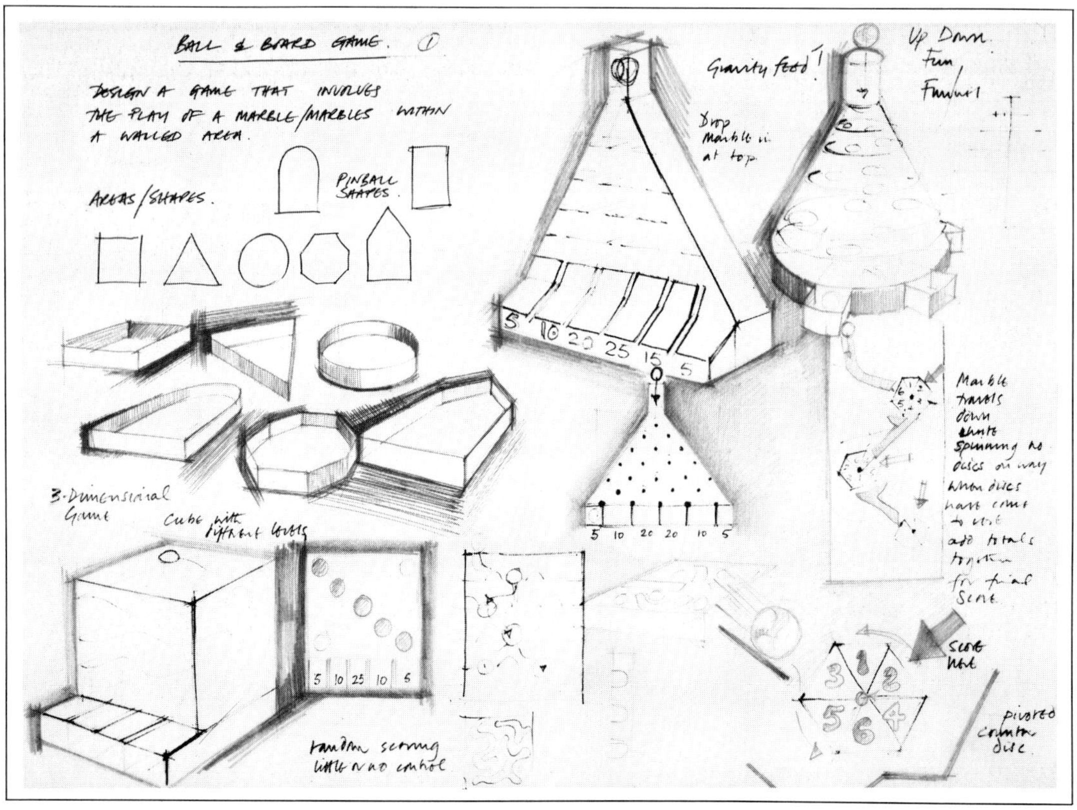

Page from a sketchbook

▸ SIGNS, SYMBOLS AND LOGOS

Sometimes information needs to be communicated in a simple and bold way. **Signs** and **symbols** give information quickly and, quite often, without the need for words.

Large companies such as British Telecom use a type of symbol called a **logo** as a means of rapid identification. The use of colour is important in many signs, symbols and logos.

▸ DIAGRAMS

Diagrams can show us how something works or give instructions on how to do something.

They may use a combination of words and pictures, pictures by themselves or, as in a circuit diagram, symbols.

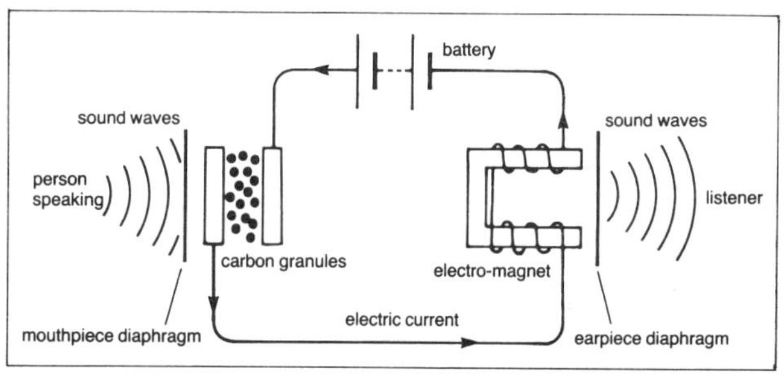

How a phone works

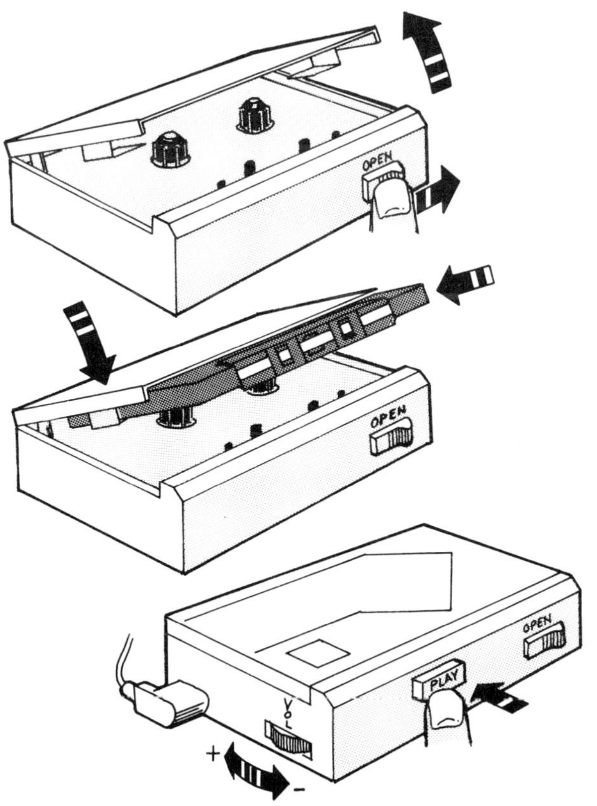

How to load a cassette into a personal stereo

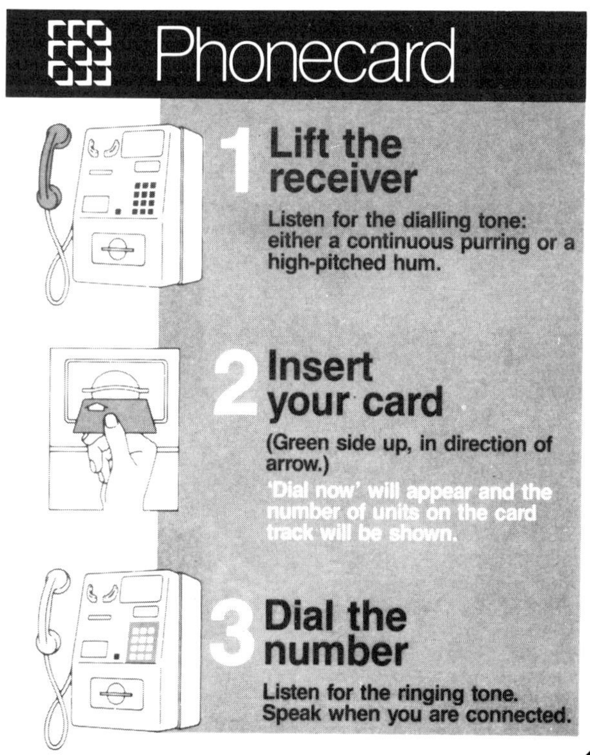

How to use a Phonecard call box

▸ MODELS

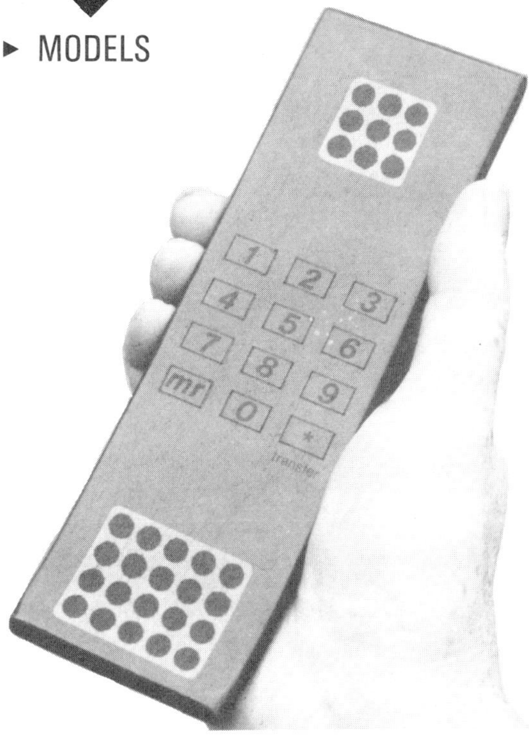

Models can be thought of as 'three-dimensional drawings' which help to communicate our ideas in a more realistic way than a two-dimensional design. They can be used at an early stage to help work out ideas, or they can be highly-finished to look like the final design solution. They may also be used to demonstrate how something works.

▸ PRESENTATION DRAWINGS

These are carefully-produced drawings which represent the final design. They can be drawn in **perspective** to give the impression of depth, and they may be **rendered** to show the textures and colours of the materials that make up the design.

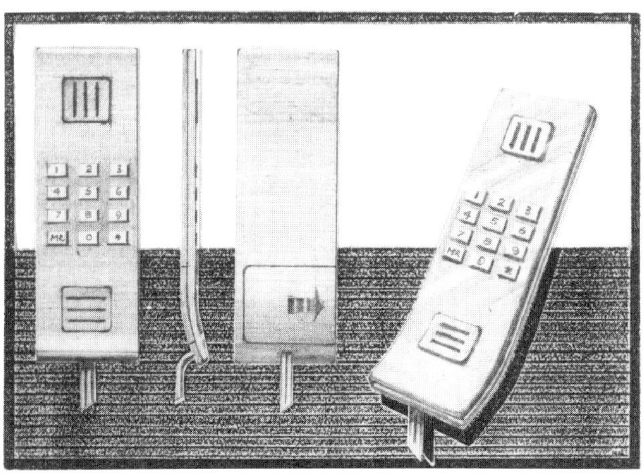

Exploded views and **sections** can also be used for presentation purposes to give an idea of how an object fits together or what is inside it.

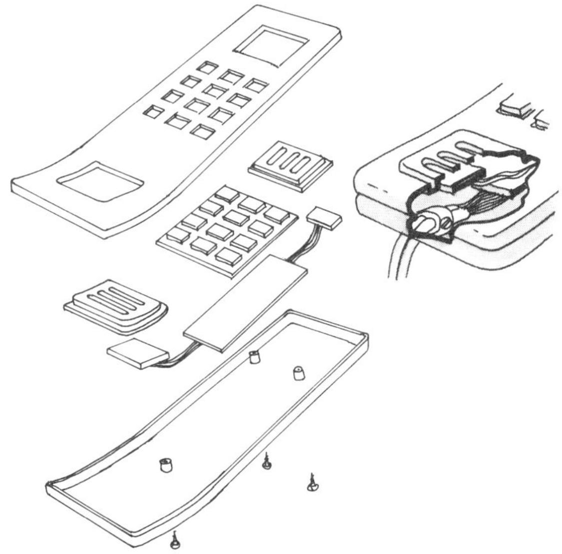

▸ PRODUCTION DRAWINGS

These are very accurate drawings which are specially-prepared so that they show all the details needed in order to make the final design.

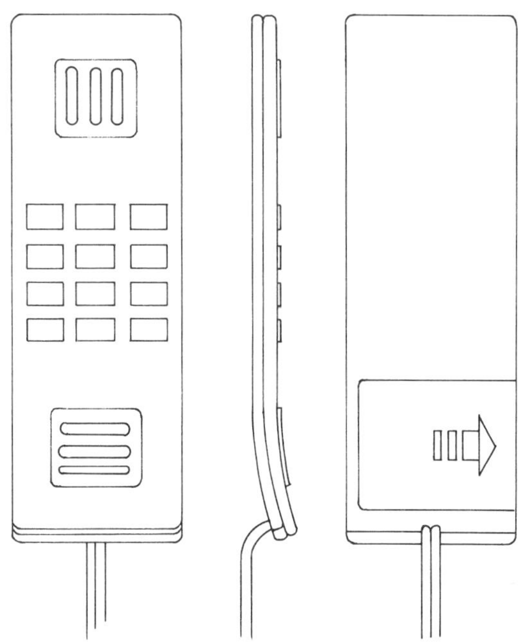

The way you present all your drawings is very important. You will find more details about presentation on pages 85–87.

▸ 'I CAN'T DRAW.' *OH YES YOU CAN!*

If you can hold a pencil, you can draw. Drawing is simply putting marks on to a surface and it has to be learned, like learning to write the alphabet. You have to learn a new **visual language** of drawing techniques and combine them with observation.

Drawing involves more than just using a pencil and your hand. Your eyes send messages to your brain and your brain tells your hand how and what to draw. Your brain is your own personal computer and, like all computers, it is only as good as the information which it contains.

So the key to drawing is careful observation of the world around you. Gradually, your confidence and technique will improve and you will develop greater **visual awareness**.

Drawing involves using your eyes, brain and hand

instead of just doodling try looking and drawing what you see

▸ WHERE DO I GET IDEAS?

Few designs are completely new. Most are the result of developments in technology, which lead to improvements in existing designs.

Style affects the visual or **aesthetic** appearance of an article. Styles change for a variety of reasons, such as the development of materials like plastics which can be moulded into almost any imaginable form. The microchip has allowed electrical articles to be miniaturized. Energy conservation, safety and the desire to travel faster have changed the form of the car.

Careful *observation* and *research* together with a good scrapbook will help you to develop good design ideas. Research is one of the most important aspects of design.

This digital watch uses a micro-chip

Starting out

BASIC MEDIA

It is not necessary to have expensive materials to start Design and Communication. All you need are paper, pencils, a sharpener, an eraser and a fine line fibre tipped pen.

► PAPER

Paper usually comes in a number of different sizes, called **'A' sizes**. There are also different **surfaces, weights** and **colours**. Each page of this book is A4 in size and the weight of the paper is 115 gsm (grams per square metre). The best type of paper for starting out on is thin **layout paper**, which has a smooth surface. Because you can see through layout paper, it allows you to use **underlays**, such as **grids**, to help you with your work (see page 18).

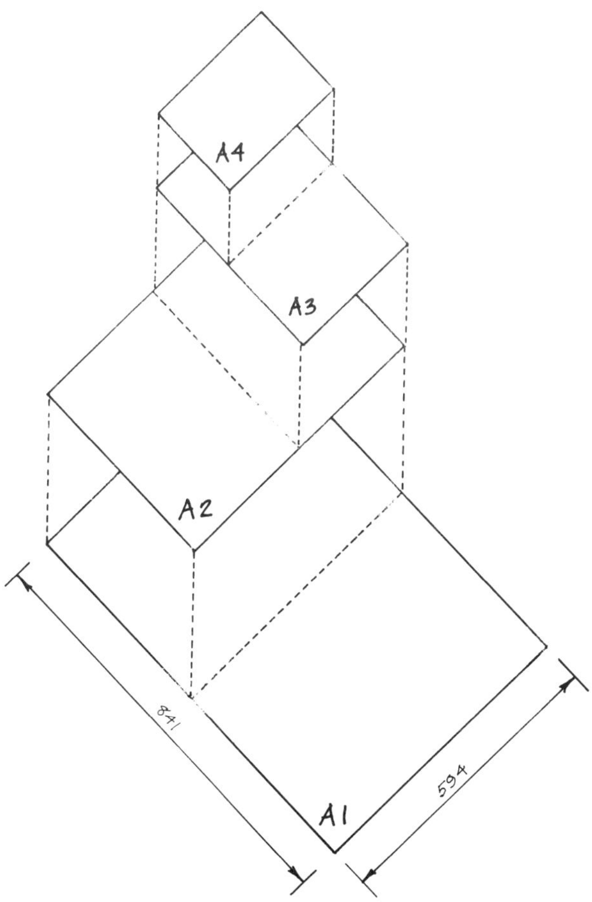

Paper sizes. A4 is half the size of A3; A3 is half of A2; A2 is half of A1

► PENCILS

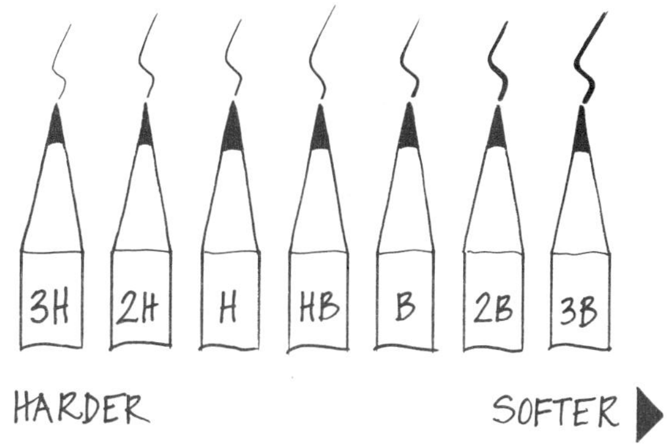

Pencil grades

Pencils are made in a wide range of grades, from very soft to very hard. The most useful grade for sketching is **2B**. This is a soft pencil—you don't have to press too heavily with it to make a mark. It can also be easily erased, if necessary. Later, when you need to make accurate production drawings, you should use a **2H** pencil. *Always keep your pencils sharp!*

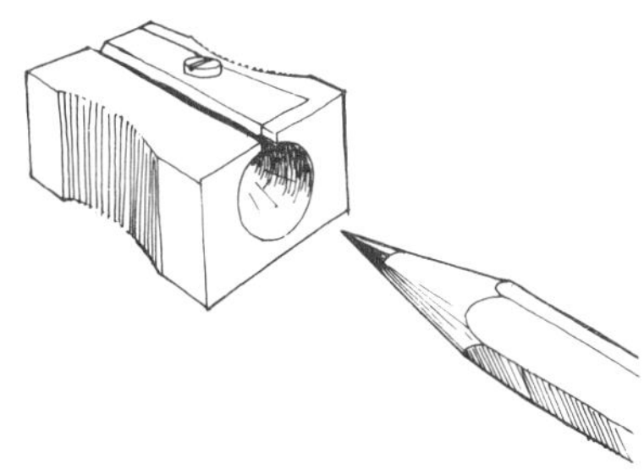

There is now a selection of **clutch** type pencils available which do not require constant sharpening. They come in a number of widths and grades of lead.

A **plastic eraser** is very useful, not only for rubbing out, but also for drawing with. (More about that technique later.)

A plastic eraser in its holder

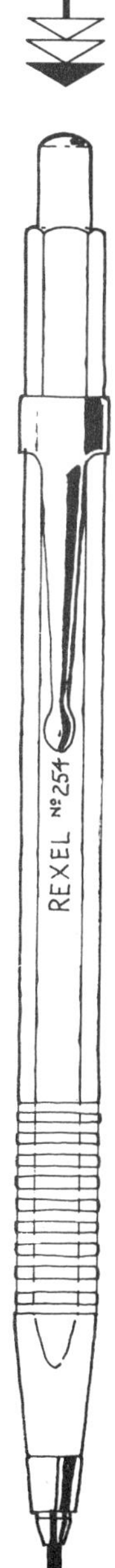

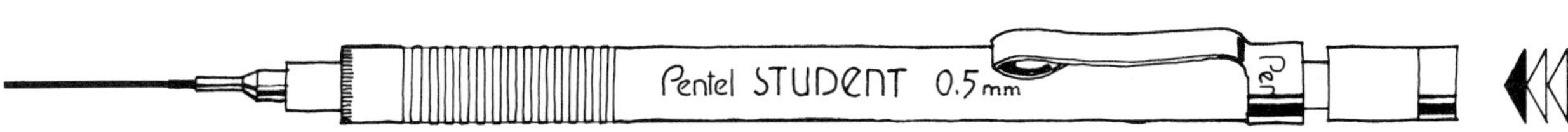

You can also try drawing with **pencil crayons** and on **coloured papers** for different effects. White-on-black is one interesting example of this technique.

A personal stereo drawn using white crayon on black paper

▸ FINE LINERS

You can make drawings using one of the many types of **fine line pens** which are now available. It is good to practise using a pen. Try to work quickly but carefully. Remember you cannot rub it out!

▸ PREPARING TO DRAW

Good preparation will help you to get better results. Make sure that you have enough room to work and also that your hands and the surface you are working on are clean. If the drawing board surface is rough, use some extra pieces of paper between your drawing and the board. It is best if you angle the board towards you at about 90° to your line of sight.

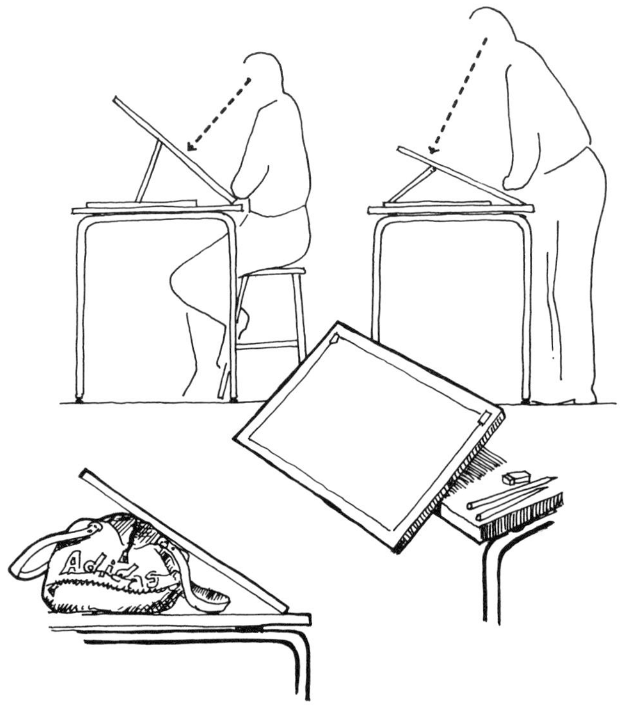

If you don't have an adjustable board, you can angle your board by resting it on your bag or the edge of a table

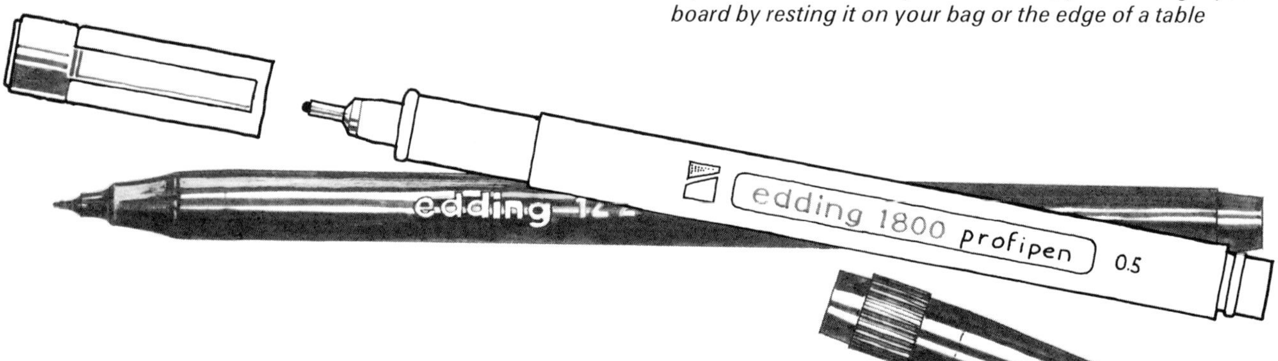

FREEHAND DRAWING

▸ WHERE TO START

There are many ways of arranging your drawings on the paper.

If you are at the stage of trying out ideas, try to work in a logical way across the paper. This will make it easier if you need to refer back to one of your drawings later. A muddled drawing will be difficult to understand.

'Now, where did I begin?'

The first marks of any drawing can often be very difficult to make, especially if the paper is white. Try not to draw too close to the edge of the paper. Be bold and don't worry if it doesn't look right at first—you can always try again on a new sheet. You will gradually improve as your confidence grows. The more you practise, the more confident you will become. Practise, practise, practise!

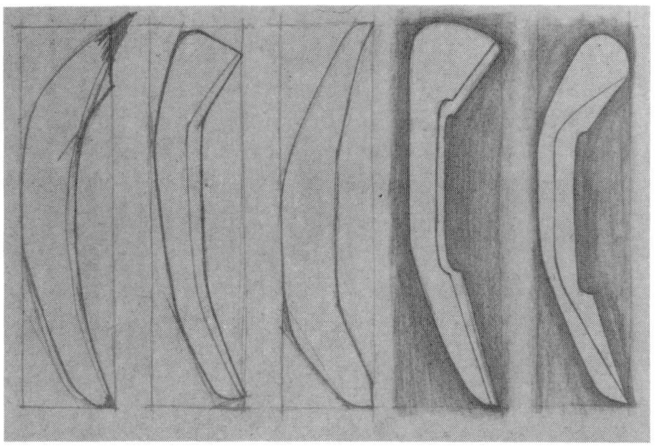

Development of ideas for the design of a telephone handset

▸ HOLDING THE PENCIL

Hold your pencil about 50 mm from the point. Do not grip it too tightly as this will make it more difficult to move the pencil freely across the paper. You can also hold the pencil at a shallow angle to draw a thicker line or to shade an area.

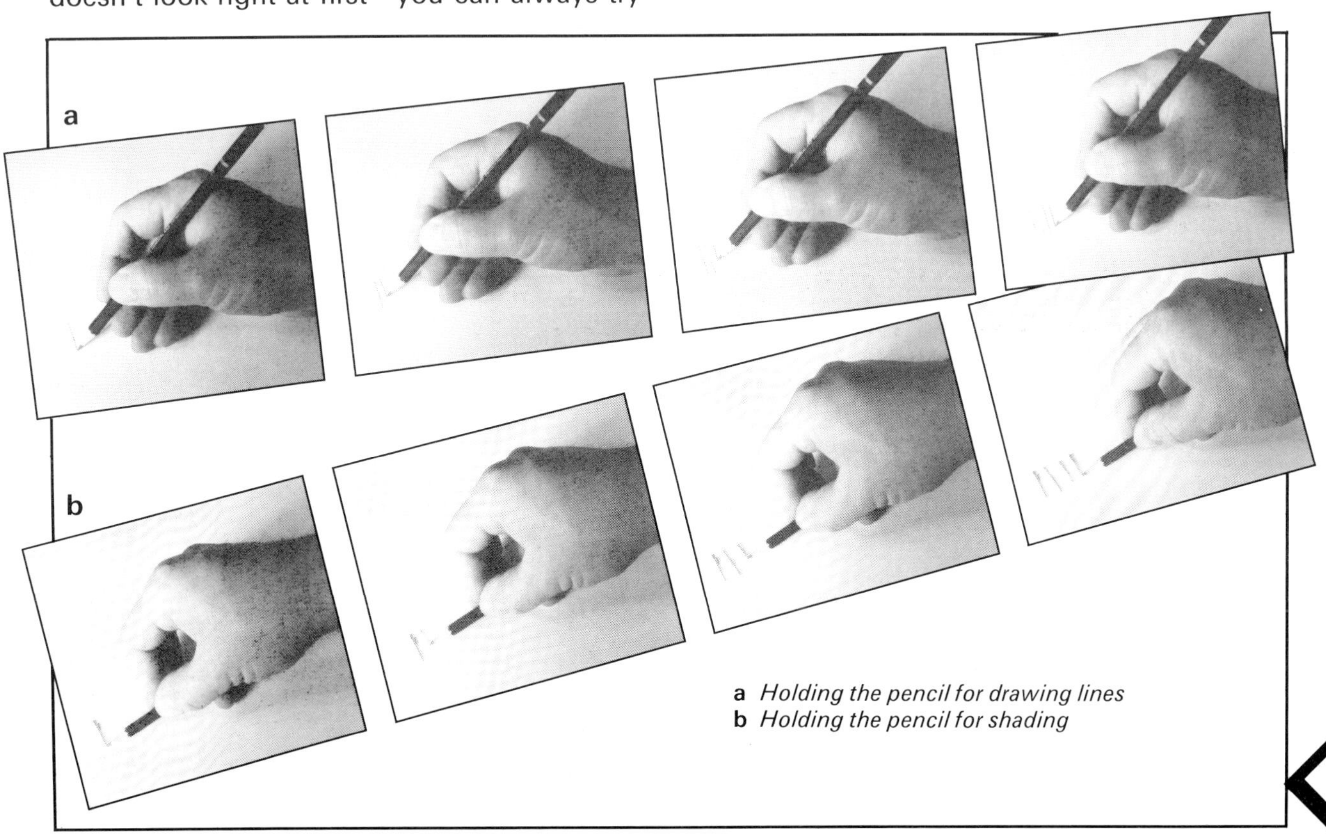

a *Holding the pencil for drawing lines*
b *Holding the pencil for shading*

LINES

Every day, we use lines in many hundreds of different ways. Handwriting uses lines to make up letters and words. Each page of this book has a border line around it. The words on this page are in lines. When designers plan a page of a book or pamphlet, they often use lines to help them arrange the various items that will appear on the page.

Lines and linear designs are all around you. The photographs on this page show you just a few examples.

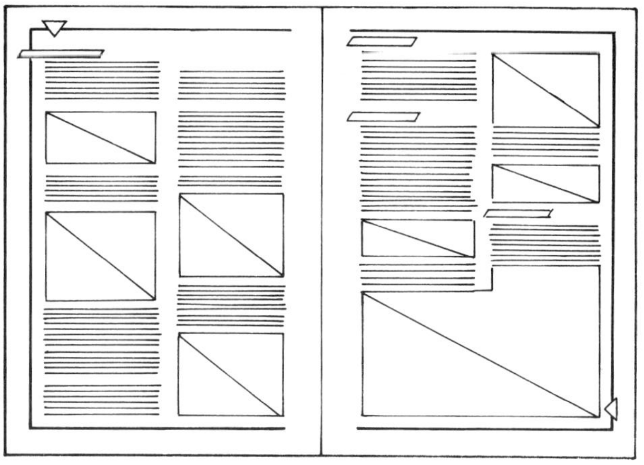

Lines were used to help design this book

Tree branches

Rock strata

A spider's web

Steel girders

Roofing panels

Assignment: *Look at, and make drawings of, as many examples of linear designs as you can find from home, school, in town, in the garden, etc. Collect photographs from magazines and keep them in your scrapbook.*

▸ STRAIGHT LINES

To draw straight lines freehand, keep your wrist locked so that you move your whole arm across the paper with each stroke you make. If you are right-handed, draw horizontal lines from left to right; if you are left-handed, draw from right to left.

Draw vertical lines from top to bottom. Practise drawing the three types of straight line. Draw them close together, spaced apart, feint to heavy.

Hold your pencil at a shallow angle and draw some broad lines. Experiment to see what effects you can achieve with different lines. Use a fine liner as well.

▸ CURVED LINES

To draw long curved lines, you must keep your wrist locked as you did for straight lines, but instead of moving your whole arm across the page, you should use your elbow as a pivot.

To draw tighter curves, you can flex your wrist, moving your hand only. Practise a variety of different lines with both pencil and fine liner.

If you use a pencil on its side, you can shade a large area and then use an eraser to *rub in* lines.

Erased lines

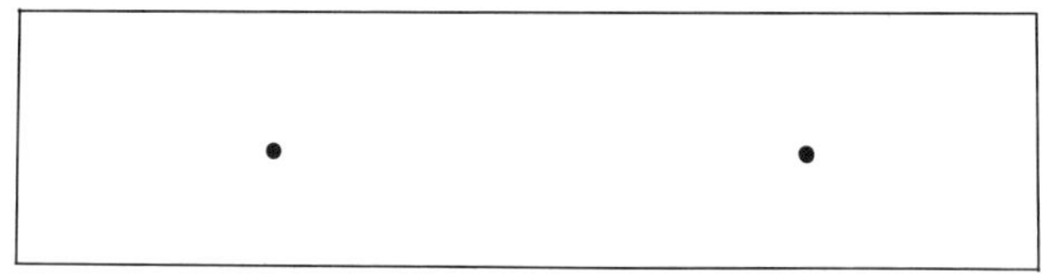

If you place two points on a piece of paper, your mind tends to connect them with an **imaginary line**; and when you draw something, you can relate points to each other by joining them with lines to make an image. For example, a contour line on a map joins together points which are the same height above sea level.

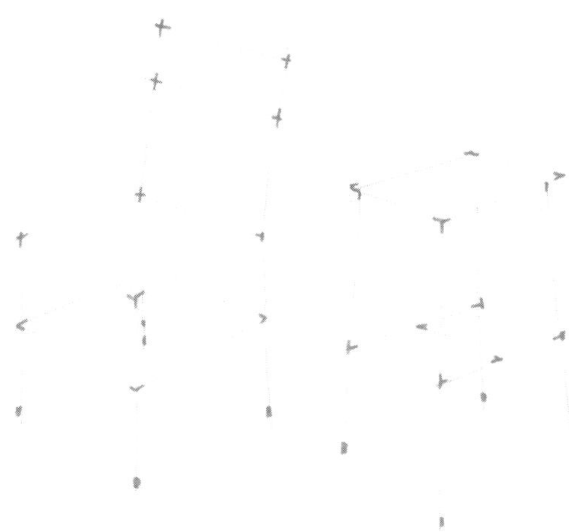

The points can be joined together, to give a chair and a stool

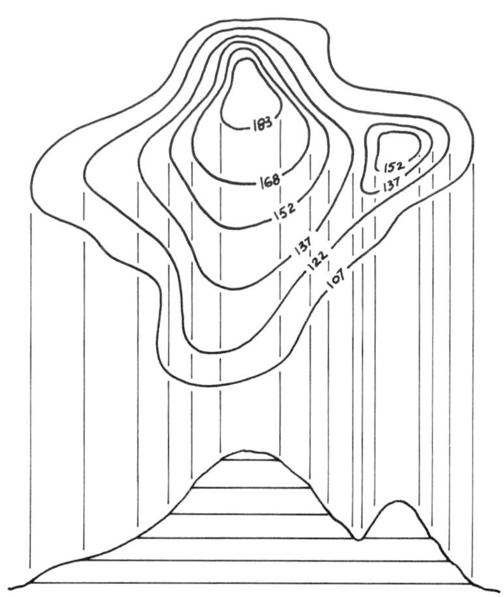

Contour lines join up points of equal height, as shown on the section through two hills above

Lines can be **thick, thin, straight, curved, heavy, feint, dashed** or **dotted**.

SHAPE

Remember the two points and the imaginary line that joins them? If you add another point, it suggests a triangle, and if you add one more point, you have a quadrilateral such as a square.

When you join up points with a line in this way, you create a **shape** in **outline**. Try drawing a variety of straight-sided shapes using points. Make your lines pass through the points a little—this will give you more freedom.

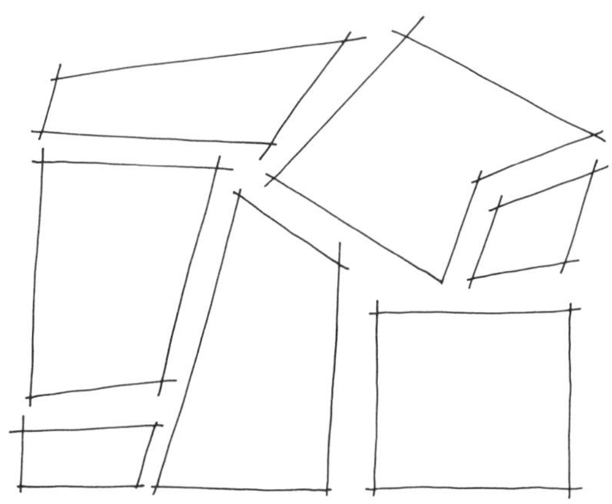

Curved shapes, such as circles, are harder to draw. When drawing a circle, make several light circles without taking your pencil off the paper. Then pick the most accurate one and draw it in more heavily. If you have problems, try fitting the circle into a square.

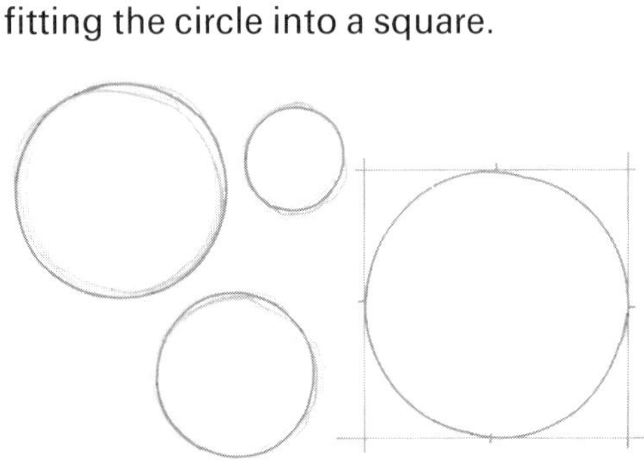

If you use a square, make the circle touch each side

Shapes can be divided into two general groups; **geometric** and **random**. Some shapes are also **symmetrical**, which means that if they are divided by a centre line, each half is exactly the same. Fold a piece of paper in half and then use scissors to cut out a shape along the fold line. When you unfold the cut out paper, the two halves will be the same. You have created a symmetrical shape.

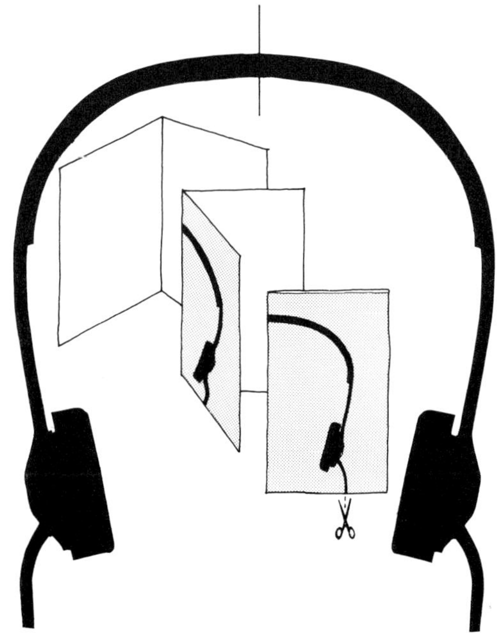

The headphones are symmetrical. One side was cut out along the fold line

▸ WHAT? NO OUTLINE?

So far, you have been drawing using outlines, but you can also draw shapes using lines in other ways. Try drawing some shapes made up of horizontal, vertical or diagonal lines. Experiment with thick and thin lines and try both pencil and pen. Try circles as well, but don't draw an outline first! There are many examples of lines used in this way, especially in logos.

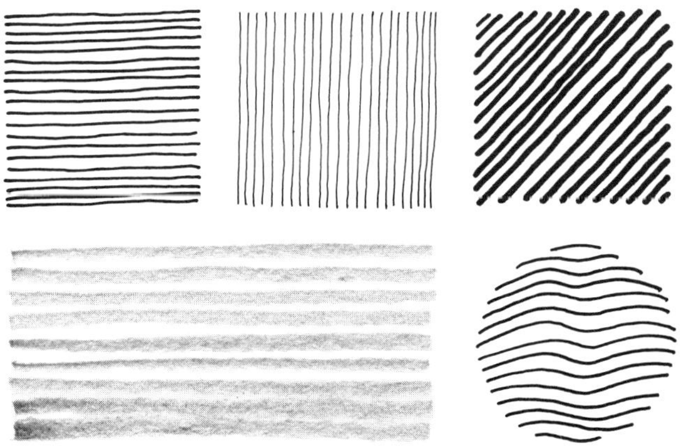

The 'Lynx' Transport logo uses horizontal lines to create the shape of the animal

Letterforms created using lines without outline

***Assignment**: Design a logo / symbol which is made up of lines, but which does not have an outline, for one of the following:*

1 *a sports shop*
2 *an optician*
3 *a garden centre*
4 *a pet shop*
5 *a record shop*

Think about a name for the shop, and use objects which you would find on sale there as the basis for the symbol.

USING SHAPE

Shape is **two-dimensional**. It has a length and a breadth but no depth and relates only to **surface area**. There are a variety of ways in which you can use shape to good effect in your design work.

▸ SHAPES TO WORK WITHIN: GRIDS

For centuries, artists and designers have used grids to help them work out their designs. Grids can take many shapes, but perhaps the most useful is the **square grid**. The square grid can be used for **enlarging** and **reducing**, as a basis for **pattern** and as a **graph** to record information.

Patterned furnishings designed using a grid

Grids can be made up of other shapes such as triangles and rectangles. There are also grids which help with **perspective drawing**. (Perspective drawing is a way of creating the impression of depth on a two-dimensional surface. This is explained later. See page 29.)

Used as an **underlay**, grids can help you to organize the positions of your drawings in relation to each other in much the same way as you use a lined underlay in a pad of notepaper.

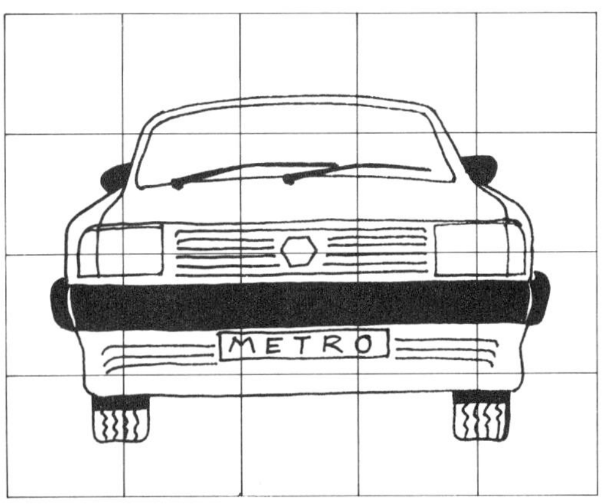

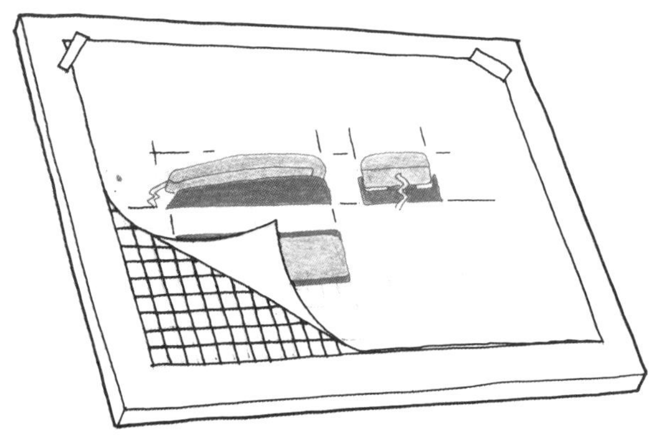

Using an underlay grid

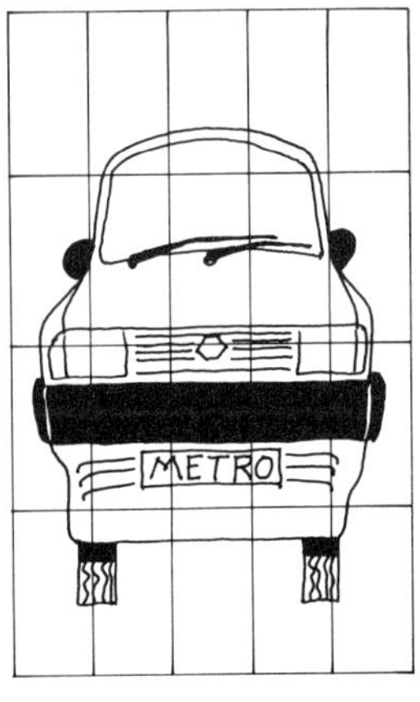

You can also use a grid to distort an image

How have these distorted images been created?

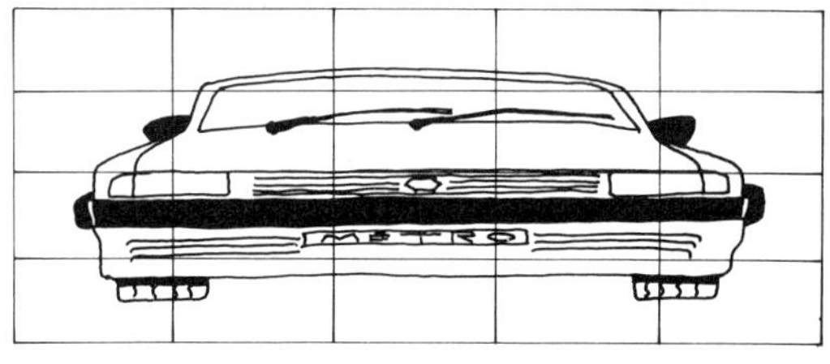

▸ PATTERN

A **pattern** is usually made up of shapes arranged on a surface, but sometimes an arrangement of *objects* can also form a pattern. Pattern is all around you. The photographs on this page show some examples. Some patterns are geometrical, some are random.

In a pattern, the same shape may be repeated, or a number of different shapes may be used. Quite often, a **repeating pattern** will fit into a grid. In some examples, such as tiles and bricks, the grid is formed by the edge of each unit of the pattern.

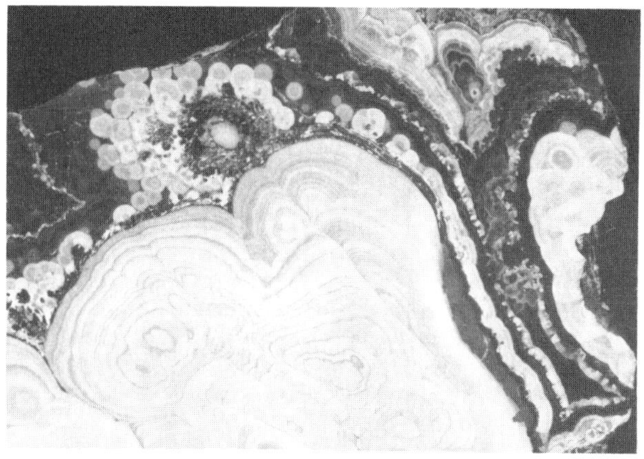

A section of the mineral malachite

Brickwork creates a repeating pattern

The roof of an aircraft hanger

Aerial photograph of roads and fields

Tree bark

A tyre tread

The Giant's Causeway, Northern Ireland—a pattern of basalt columns

Which of the above patterns are man-made and which are natural? Which are geometric and which are random?

Assignment: *Look for examples of pattern and record them in your scrapbook or sketchbook. Use tracing paper over them to work out if they are based on a grid.*

A shape that is repeated to make a pattern is called a **motif**. A motif can be repeated in several ways. For example, it can be placed side by side, mirrored, half-dropped or turned through 90°. Each of these will produce a different effect.

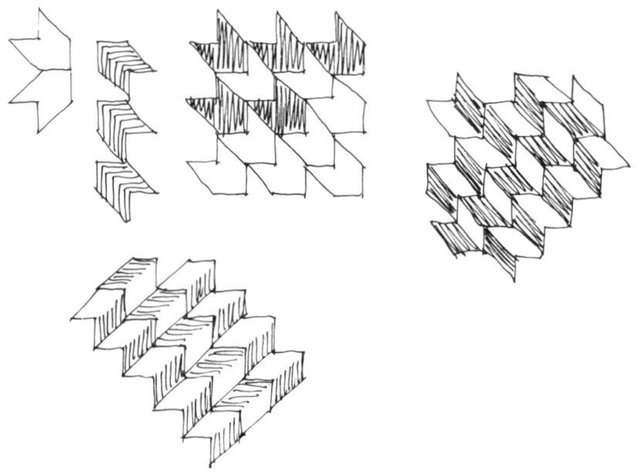

Ways of repeating a motif

The Herman Grid is a pattern of squares which creates an optical illusion. What seems to happen when you look at the white intersections between the squares?

When you make a pattern, you will produce **positive** and **negative** shapes. The motif can be thought of as the positive shape. Negative shapes are created around it. Many optical effects can be produced in this way.

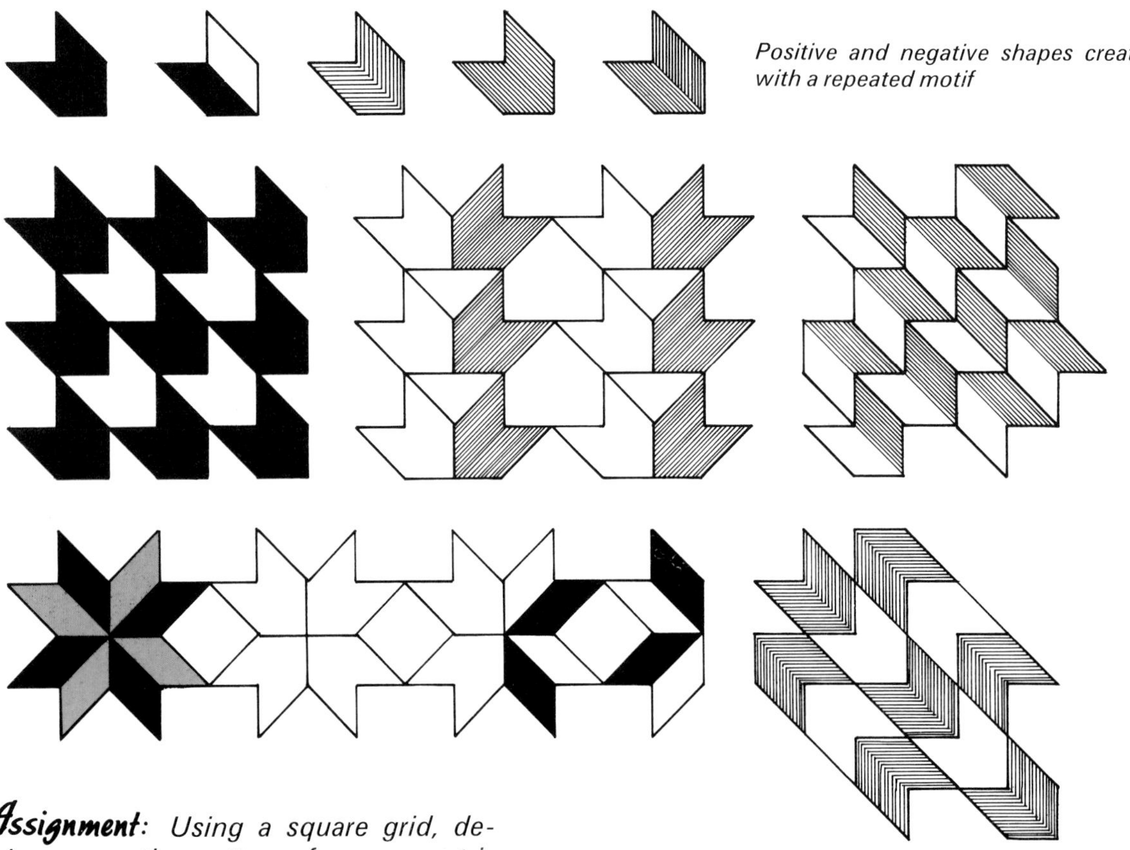

Positive and negative shapes created with a repeated motif

Assignment: *Using a square grid, develop a repeating pattern of one geometric motif to produce a positive and negative effect. The pattern is to be used for wrapping paper and bags for a gift shop. See page 46 for some coloured patterns.*

Patterns can also be derived from natural forms (objects) such as fruit, vegetables, shells, etc. If you make a carefully-observed drawing of a natural form and then isolate a part of it using a small **window** of card or paper, the section you have picked out can be **simplified** and **repeated** to produce another pattern. This technique is called **abstraction**.

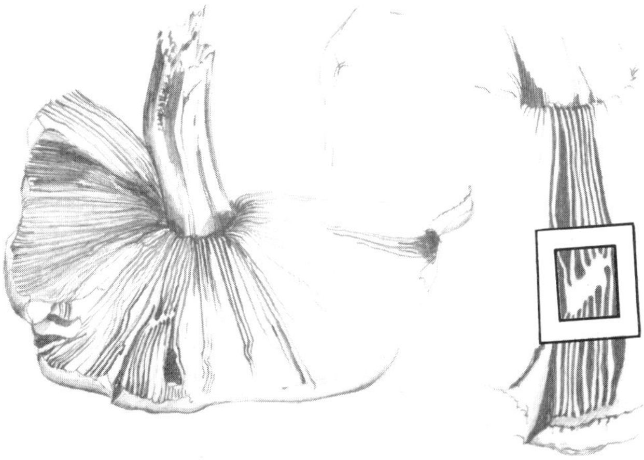

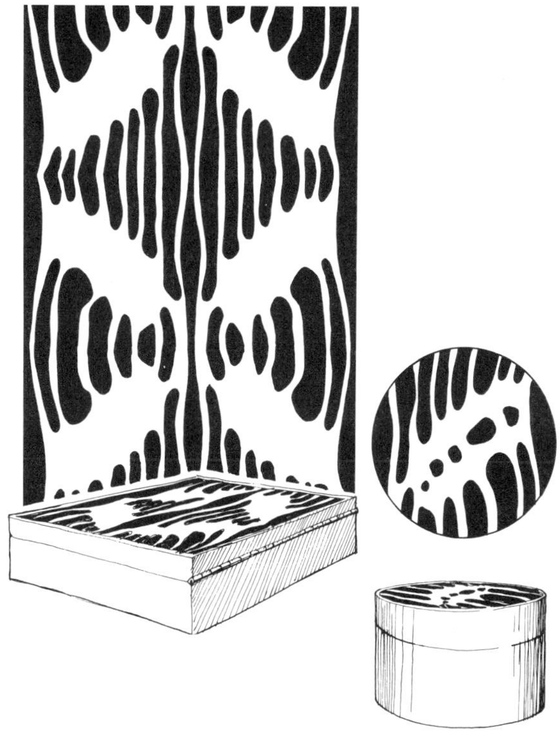

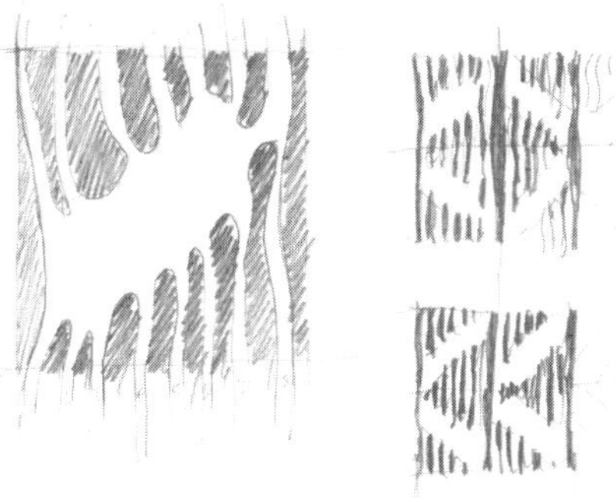

This design is developed from a drawing of a mushroom, and could be enamelled or cast with resin on the lids of the boxes

Man-made objects, such as cars or buildings, can also be used to develop abstract patterns, and the careful use of colour will create different effects.

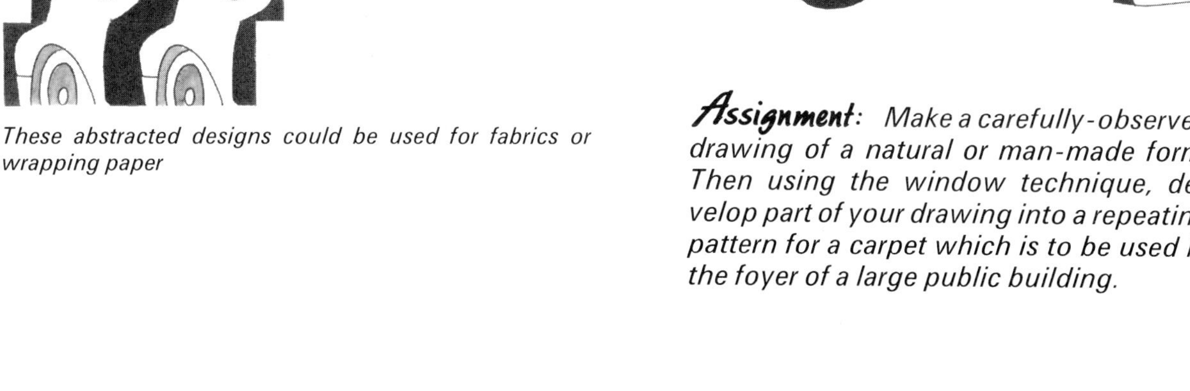

These abstracted designs could be used for fabrics or wrapping paper

Assignment: *Make a carefully-observed drawing of a natural or man-made form. Then using the window technique, develop part of your drawing into a repeating pattern for a carpet which is to be used in the foyer of a large public building.*

▸ BOUNDARY SHAPES

Comic strips are one example of shape being used as a **boundary**. The shapes in a comic strip are usually all the same height, but may vary greatly in width. This could be thought of as a **random grid**. Some parts of the drawing may even break across the boundary shapes.

Assignment: *Using shapes of the same height but different width, produce a comic strip to illustrate either a short passage from a book of your choice, or a good joke.*

Shapes can also be used in a similar way to house diagrams which give step by step instructions for certain tasks. Diagrams of this kind should always be simple and straightforward so as not to confuse. Quite often, they are purely visual and use no written information at all.

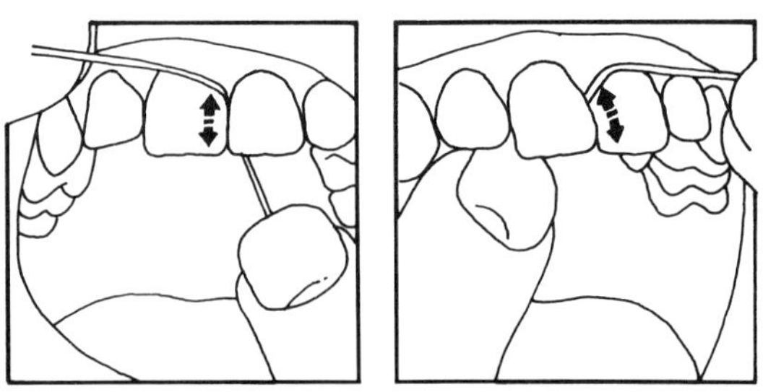

Step by step instructions for using dental floss

Assignment: *Choose a simple job or task and write down a list of the stages involved to complete it. Then make simple, bold drawings of the stages and fit them into shapes in a logical sequence. Use squared paper as an underlay sheet to help. Draw out your final design accurately and get a friend to test and evaluate it. Does it do the job? Is it too complicated?*

Shapes can be useful in working out designs for objects. For example, in the sketches below a rectangle has been used to work out the **side view** of a pull-along toy. Using a pale colour, the shapes have been made to stand out from the background. The chosen design has been picked out using a different shade and other shapes have then been used to draw the object from two more positions: the **end** and the **plan views**. These three views are called **elevations**.

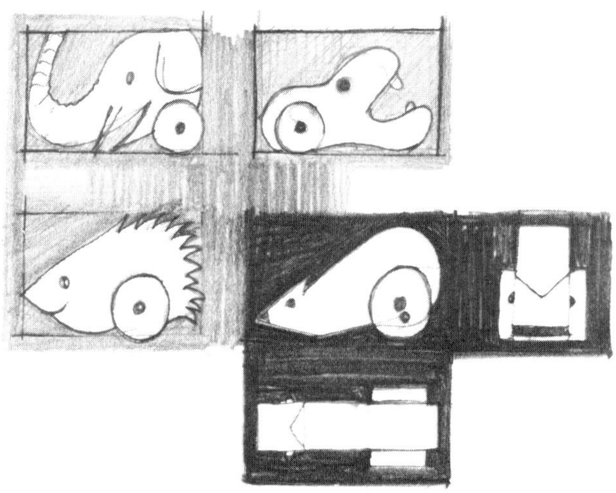

Sketch designs using elevations for a pull-along toy

Assignment: *Using a rectangular shape, work out designs for your own pull-along toy. You could base your designs on animals or transport. A square underlay grid will help you.*

Drawing an object using elevations is called **orthographic projection** and there are two methods that you can use. These are **first angle projection** and **third angle projection**. You will notice that the positions of the elevations are different for each method.

▶ FIRST ANGLE

If you imagine the object you wish to draw inside a glass box, the elevations will be projected back onto the sides of the box. If the box was opened out, the elevations would lie on a flat surface. As you can see, six elevations are possible, but we can usually manage with three.

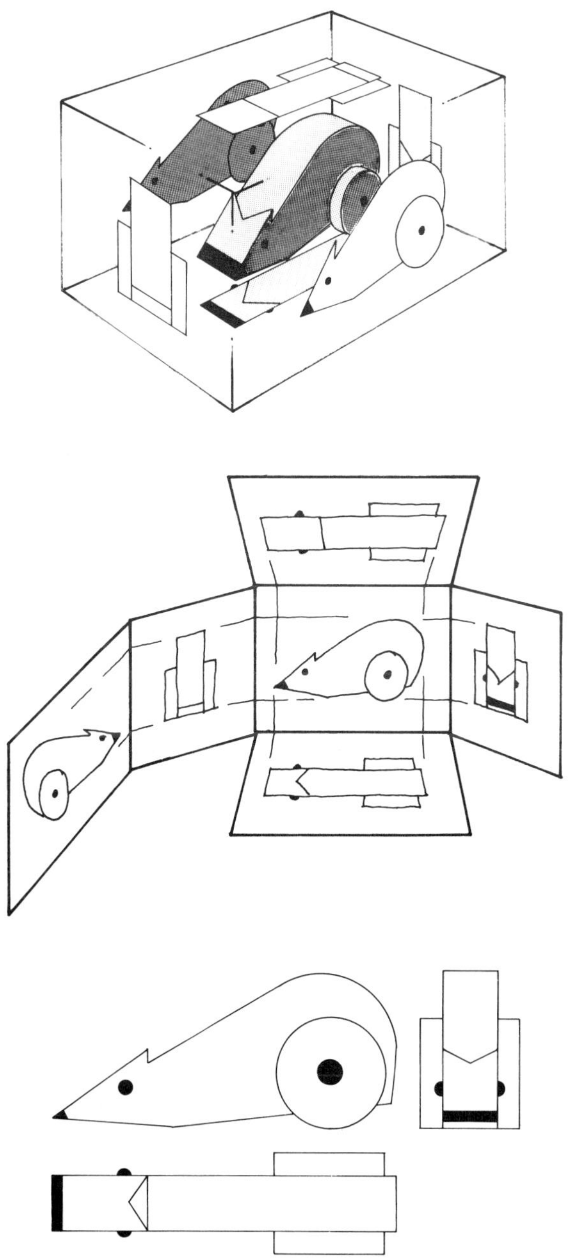

First angle projection

▶ THIRD ANGLE

Imagine the object inside the glass box again, but this time think of the elevations projected towards the surface *nearest* to them. Again, if the box is opened out, there are six possible elevations.

Look carefully at the different positions of the elevations of the toy mouse in first and third angle projection. Can you suggest any ways to help you remember which is which? Which elevation stays in the same position for both methods?

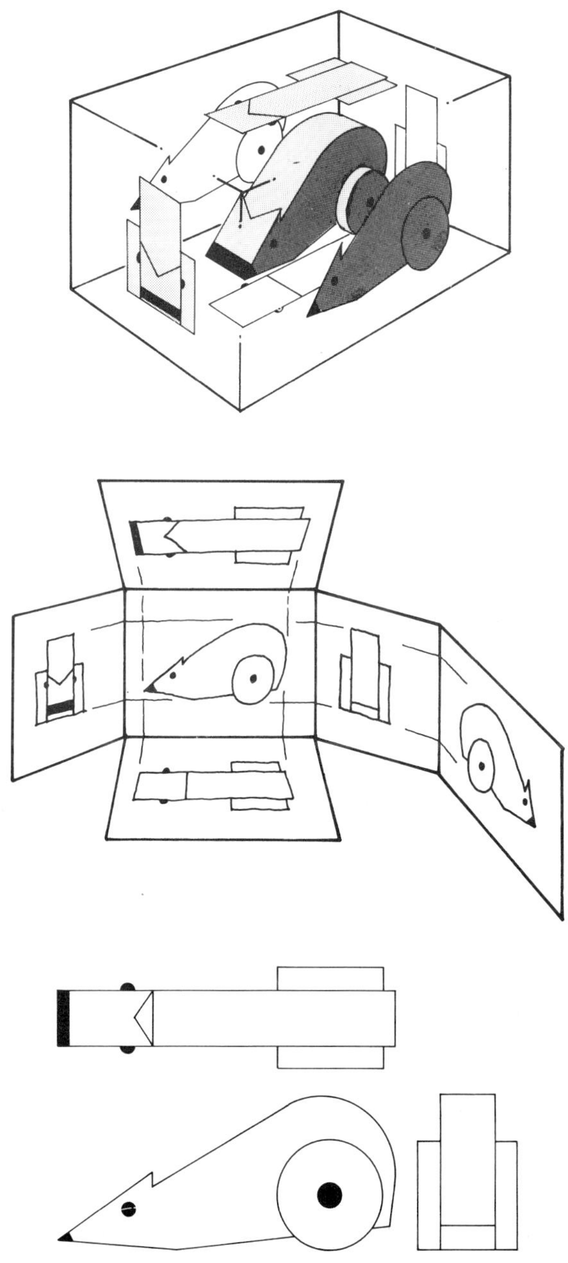

Third angle projection

At present, you will only be concerned with freehand orthographic drawing. Later in the book, more accurate, measured orthographic drawing will be introduced.

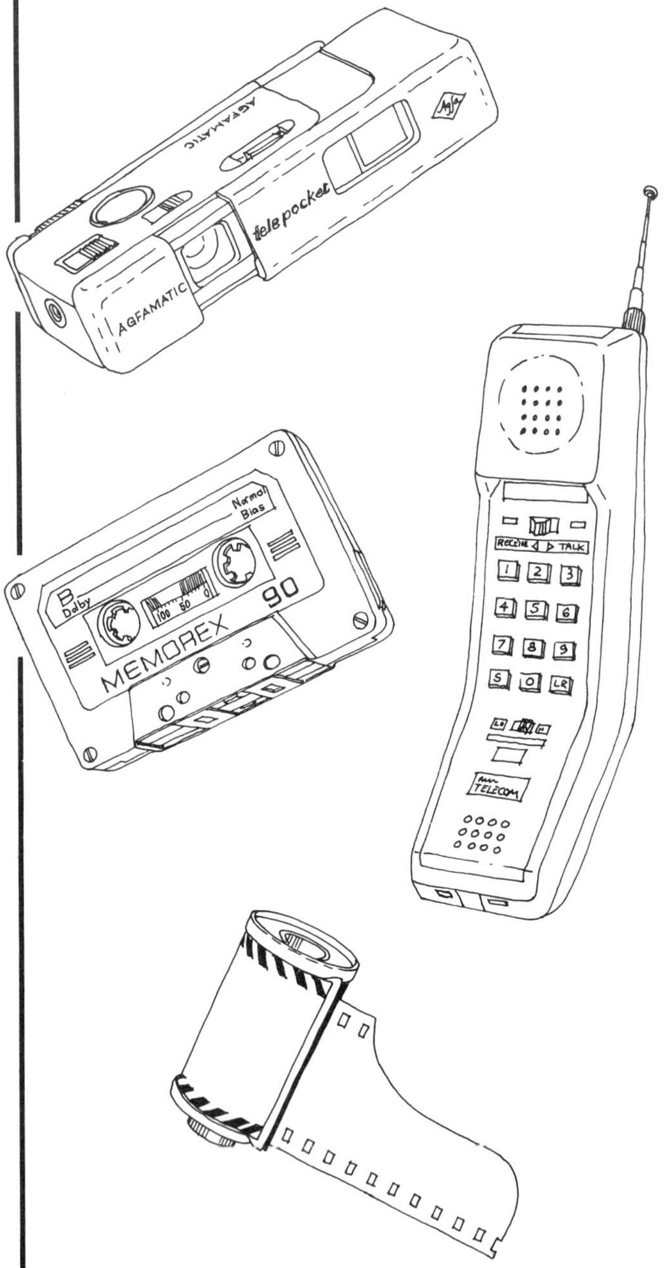

Assignment: *Above, you will find several examples of objects in everyday use. Make freehand orthographic drawings of each of them. Do some in first angle and some in third angle. Use an underlay grid to help you position each elevation correctly.*

▸ THE SAME SIZE OR NOT THE SAME SIZE?

Look at the drawings in the rectangles and circles below. They all show objects of vastly different size, but the rectangles and circles which contain them are all the *same* size. In other words, the **scale** of each drawing is different.

Some objects are **scaled up** to larger than life size, others are **scaled down** to a smaller size. Only one of each shape is **full size**. (Which ones are they?) Scale can be used to create the impression of depth in your drawings.

Assignment: *Draw several identical shapes and then make them look like objects of different sizes. See how many different variations you and your friends can come up with. You can use side views or plan views.*

▸ SHAPES IN SPACE

Overlapping and reducing

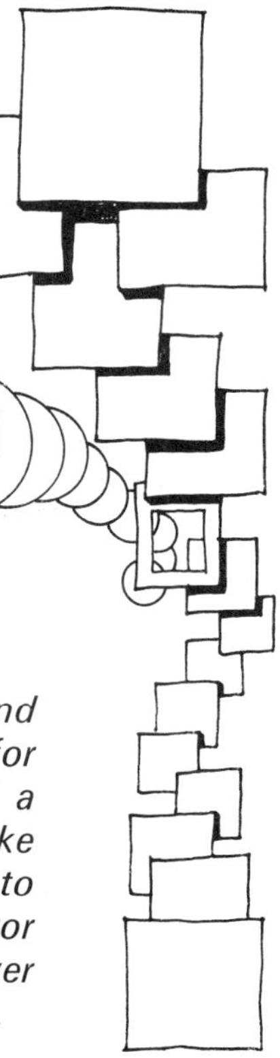

Although shapes are flat and have no depth, we can create an impression or **illusion** of depth and scale by **overlapping** and **reducing** the size of the shapes. Making the line where the shapes overlap slightly thicker will help to create the illusion of depth.

Try using scissors to cut out shapes so that you can position them in a number of different ways and overlap them.

If you want to use colour, make those shapes that are to be furthest away the palest. Look around you and you will see that distant objects appear to become paler and less clear.

***Assignment**: Using the overlapping and reducing technique, make a design for a mural to be placed on the wall of a shopping precinct. The mural is to make the area look larger. You may wish to consider using shapes cut out of mirror card or foil. Mirrors are often used over walls to make small rooms appear larger.*

▸ SHAPES WHICH POINT

Shapes can be used to communicate **direction** in your drawings and diagrams. The pointing finger has been used for this purpose for many years.

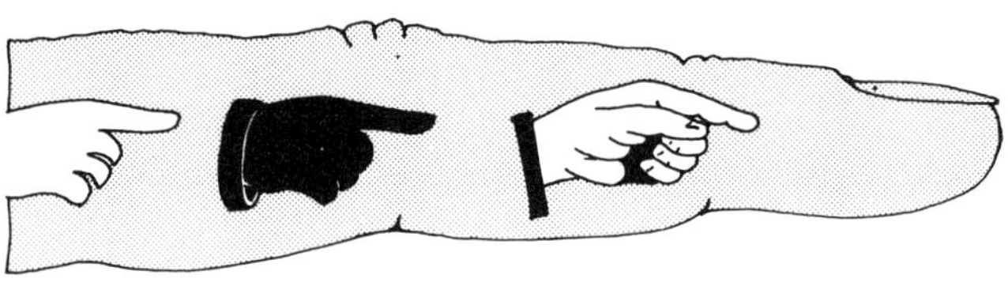

Recently, the pointing finger has given way to the **arrowhead**, which is more in keeping with modern design. It is simple and bold and therefore communicates without fear of confusion. The arrowhead can take many forms and do many jobs. It can be seen on road signs, in stations and airports, on electrically-operated equipment, in instruction manuals, etc.

An arrowhead may twist and turn to show more complicated movements. The page numbers of this book are placed in simple triangular arrowheads which lead into the page.

***Assignment**: Look around you for examples of arrows as direction indicators and either record them in your scrapbook or draw them. Practise drawing different arrows. See if you can invent your own modified arrow shapes.*

Some possible arrowhead designs

***Assignment**: Make drawings of an object that does a job by rotating, such as a drill, screwdriver or mixer. Simplify your drawings into a black and white symbol with arrows to show the directions of movement. It may help to emphasize the motion if you colour the arrows. Which colour would be best?*

LETTERING

Lettering plays an important part in design and communication in many ways. **Notes** can be made to record information and aid the development of your ideas. Printed lettering can be used for **labels** and **headings**. Logos and packages may use stylized letter forms.

If you look carefully at the letters of the alphabet, you will see that they are made up of lines and shapes. Some letters are made up only of straight lines, some letters are only curved lines and some are a combination of straight and curved. Letters may enclose shapes or they may just consist of lines with no enclosed region.

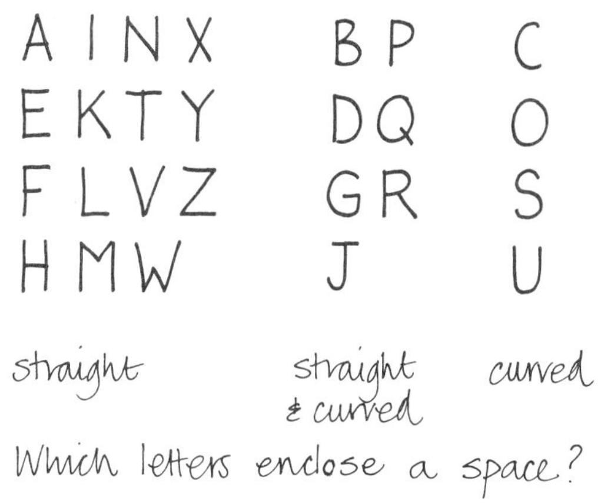

You will notice that not all letters have vertical edges—some are wider at the top than at the bottom, and vice versa. You must make allowances for these differences in shape when printing. Letters with vertical edges should be spaced equally. The spacing between letters which do not have vertical edges must be adjusted accordingly.

It takes practice to print letters accurately so that they give clear information. You can make life easier by using a lined underlay sheet, such as you would find in a pad of notepaper.

Make your letters fit between the lines so that they touch at the top and bottom. Look carefully at the shape and size of the letters, and keep them simple.

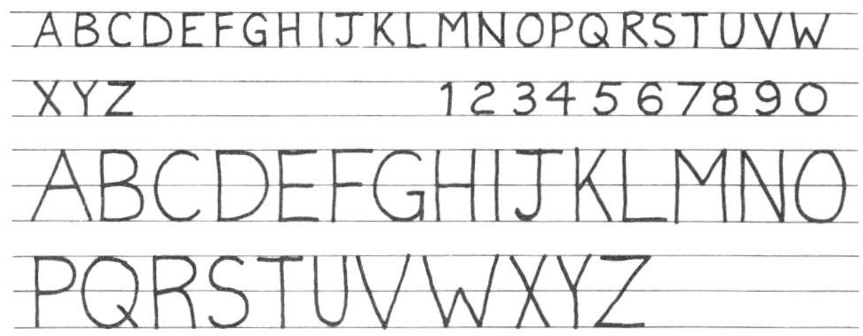

Using a lined underlay sheet

Large scale **bold** letters can be very useful in design and communication work, especially for logos and on packaging.

To build your confidence in drawing larger scale letters, try using a 10 mm grid underlay. Mark off 6 lines of the grid horizontally. Then mark off sections vertically according to the letter being drawn.

Look carefully at letter shapes: some will need more sections than others. Finally, carefully line-in the letters.

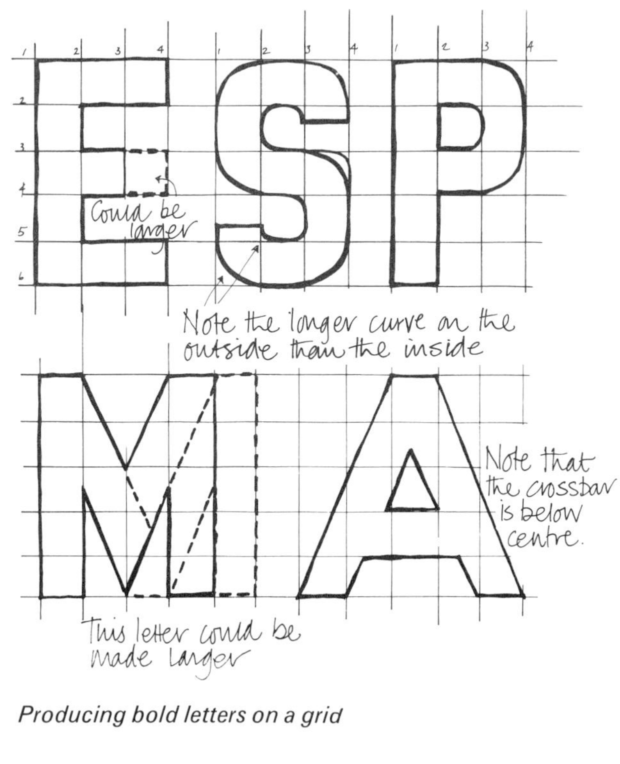

Producing bold letters on a grid

When you have practised vertical letters, you may wish to try sloping them. Remember that all lines must be parallel. *Letters that slope to the right side are called* ***italic***. They were first used in Venice, Italy to emphasize certain words in a passage of writing.

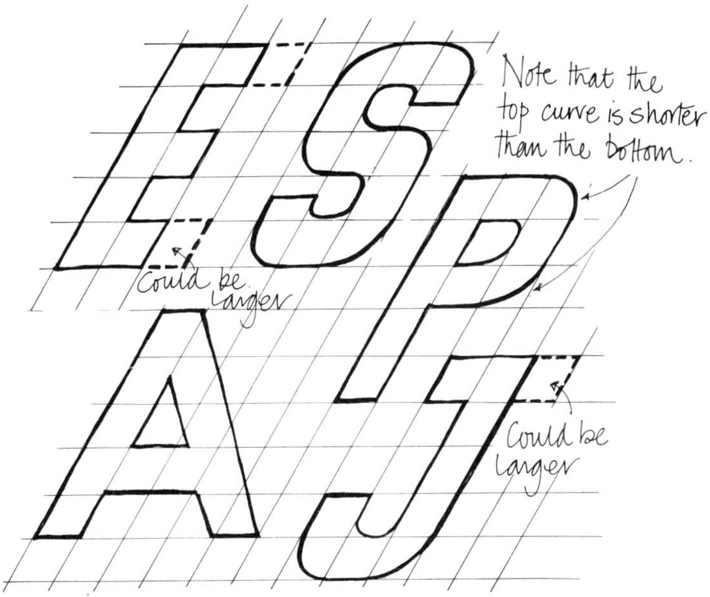

Producing italic letters on an angled grid

Lettering styles should be used to complement design work. Look at the styles and designs on this page and suggest which would work together best.

So far, you have looked at capital letters, but the same rules apply for lower case letters. If you look at a dry transfer lettering catalogue, you will see that there are hundreds of different styles. If you study them carefully, you will see that they are not too difficult to draw using the grid system.

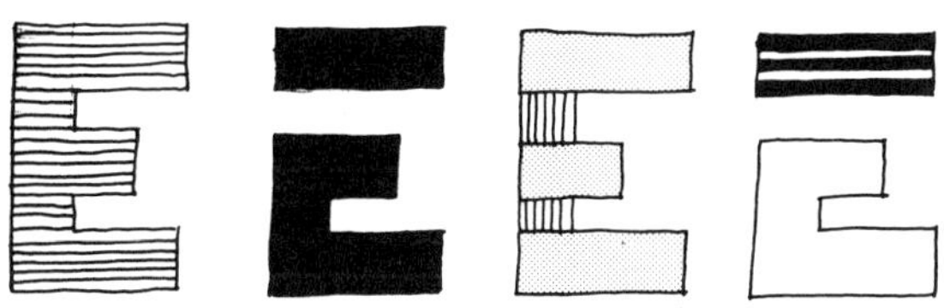

E is for experiments – try modifying letterforms BUT remember that they still have to be understood!!

BLOCK UP

L'auriol

SHATTER

Assignment: *Using letters within a geometrical shape, such as a square or rectangle, design your own personal logo. The design is to be used on all your design project folders.*

Assignment: *Choose a lettering style which you think is appropriate to one of the following TV programmes and use it to design a title caption. The caption should include some kind of visual image. This could be a pattern, a drawing or a photograph.*

1 *Tomorrows World*
2 *Top of the Pops*
3 *Wish You Were Here*
4 *Sportsnight*

The illusion of form

You have looked at the ways in which flat shapes can be used to communicate design ideas, but often you need to communicate ideas for three-dimensional objects or **forms**. How do you draw three-dimensional objects on paper so that they look realistic? You have to create an *illusion of the form* of the object.

To create the illusion of form with shape, you can use the 'overlapping' technique. A similar technique can be used in a drawing to create the illusion of a cube. The cube drawn in this way is called the **Necker Cube** after the man who first discovered it. Look first at point A and then at point B on the diagram of the Necker Cube. What seems to happen?

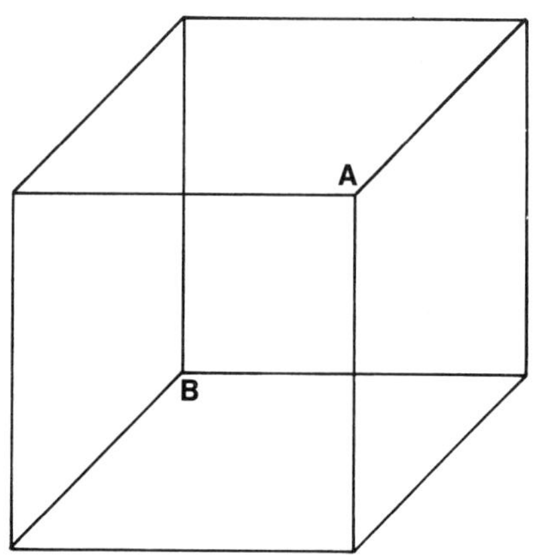

The Necker Cube

Assignment: *See if you can create the same effect using some different forms. Try them out on your friends.*

When you are designing, you do not want the form to appear to move backwards and forwards all the time. You can avoid this effect by first drawing a square with a slightly smaller square positioned behind it and drawn feintly.

Then join together only the three corners which are *outside* the first square. Erase the two lines which overlap and draw over the other lines more firmly with a pencil or fine liner. You should now have created the impression of a solid form. Try the same technique using a number of different forms. You can also use it with letters.

The method that you have just used gives the illusion of form, but does not give a true picture. To create a more accurate form, you must use **perspective**.

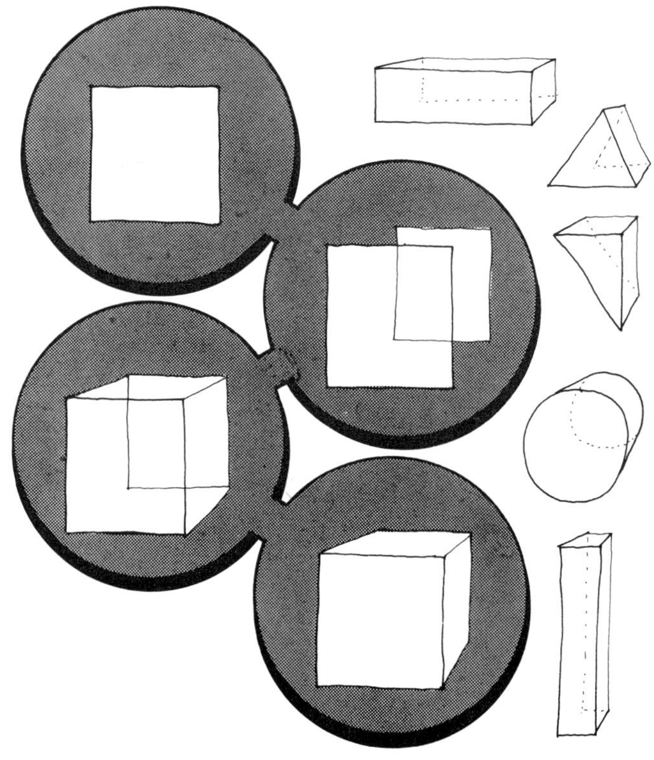

Creating the illusion of form in a drawing of a cube and, below, in lettering

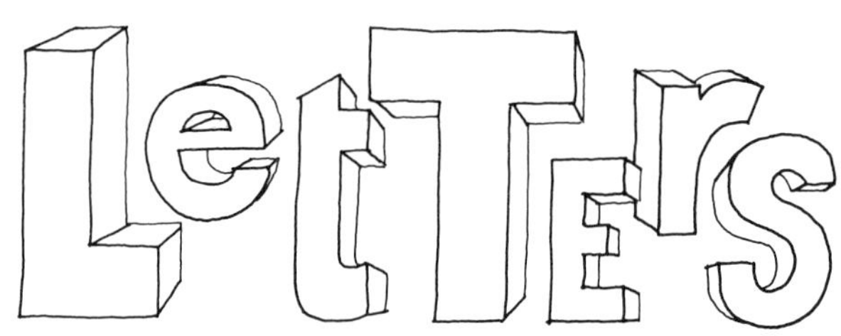

PERSPECTIVE DRAWING

When you look at an object, you do so from your **point of view**. Someone who is taller than you or, for example, standing to your side, will have a different point of view.

You also have an **eye level**, which can be thought of as an imaginary horizontal surface, level with your eyes. This imaginary surface remains horizontal even though you may look up or down.

Two points of view

As early as 500 BC, the Greeks had understood form and **foreshortening** (see below), but it was not until the Renaissance (a new period of learning and discovery that marked the start of the modern world) that an architect called Filippo Bruneleschi (1377–1446) devised a set of rules for perspective drawing.

▸ WHAT IS FORESHORTENING?

You know that all six sides of a cube are equal in size. If you hold a cube directly in front of you so that you see only one side, all the edges will appear the same length.

Now tilt the cube so that you can see both the front and the top. The top will appear *shorter* from front to back. This effect is referred to as foreshortening.

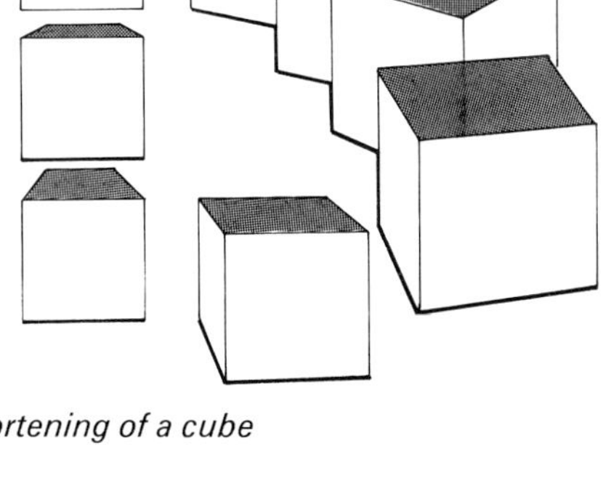

Foreshortening of a cube

▸ SINGLE POINT PERSPECTIVE

If you were standing in the middle of a road in a flat desert looking towards the horizon (the place where the land or sea appears to meet the sky), the road would seem to disappear at a point on the horizon. This is called the **vanishing point**.

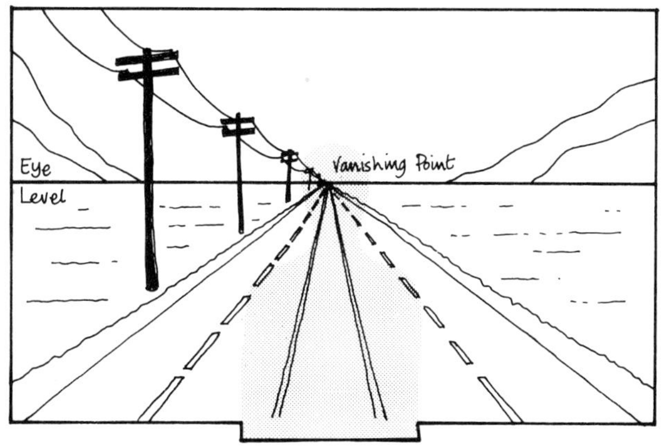

To draw in **single point perspective**, you must first draw the eye level or horizon line across your paper and then decide on your vanishing point.

Next, draw a shape below the eye level and draw feint lines from the top corners of the shape so that they meet at the vanishing point. You can then estimate the depth of the object and draw in the back edges.

If you are drawing an **angular** form, such as a **cube** or **prism**, you must make the front and back edges parallel. If you are drawing a **curved** form, you will have to make the back curve slightly smaller.

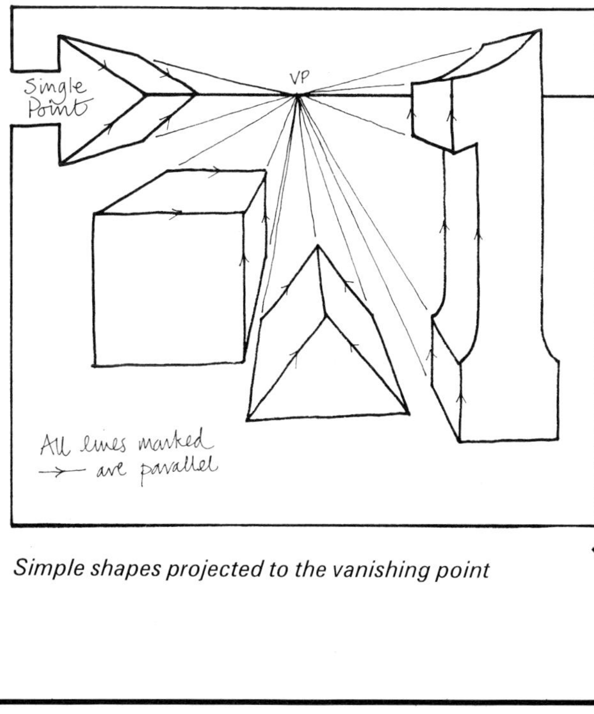

Simple shapes projected to the vanishing point

Make some drawings of simple forms, above, below and on the eye level, using this technique. Can you suggest any rules to explain which sides of an object are seen in relation to its position about the eye level and vanishing point?

Single point perspective can be used to very good effect when trying to give the illusion of depth to a drawing of a room or a street.

You can vary the position of the eye level and the vanishing point, but remember that all vertical and horizontal lines must stay parallel. You may wish to turn the paper vertically.

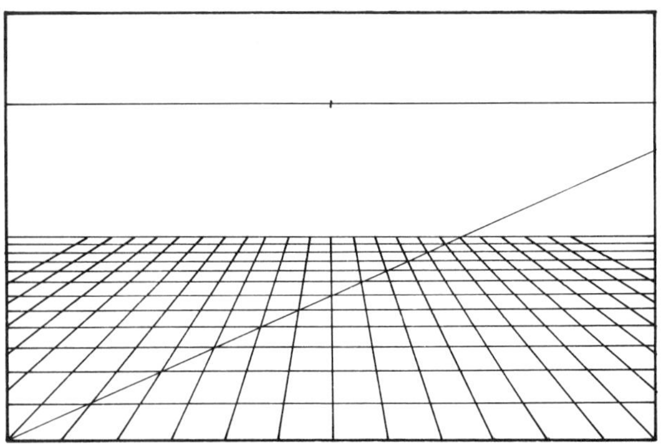

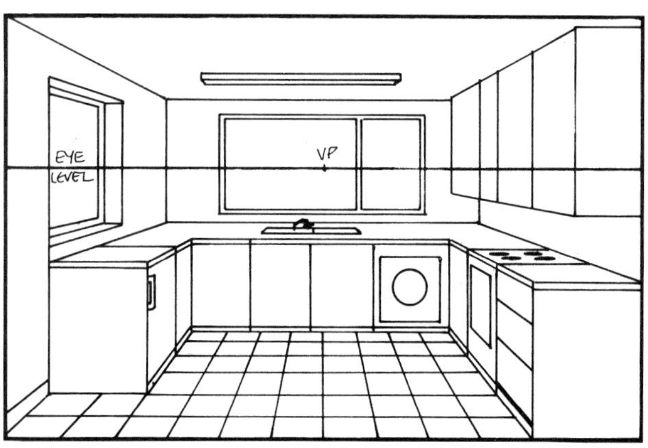

Single point perspective can be used in room planning

Assignment: *Make a carefully-observed single point perspective drawing of a room at home, such as the kitchen or bathroom. Look closely for lines that will help your drawing, such as tiles, windows and fitted units. When you have finished, lay a piece of thin layout paper over your drawing and trace off the positions of the walls, floor and ceiling. Now use this drawing to re-design the room. It will help if you do some sketches of ideas for your alterations first.*

Single point perspective can therefore be used to create the illusion of depth, but it only gives you a true image if the object is drawn directly above or below the vanishing point. If the object is drawn to one side, it becomes an impossible view.

You can prove this for yourself in the following way. Draw a horizontal line across the paper and then place the cube against it.

If you look at the cube from directly in front, you will only see one surface. If you look at it from slightly higher up, you will see both the top *and* front surfaces. In order to see three sides, you will have to *move the cube at an angle to the line*. Note: do not turn the paper itself and keep your own position fixed.

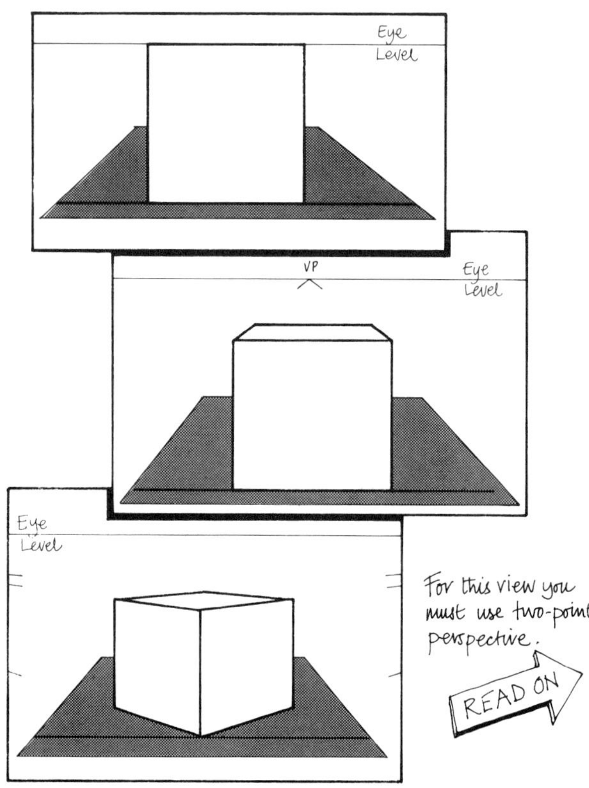

▸ TWO POINT PERSPECTIVE

In **two point perspective**, the eye level is used again, but this time there are *two* vanishing points. The two points are placed some distance apart.

Photographs can often be helpful in understanding the rules of perspective. On the photograph on this page, lines have been projected back from the building to the vanishing points in order to work out the eye level. Sometimes the vanishing points are so far apart that they will not fit on your paper. To overcome this, you can put your paper on a larger flat surface until you have drawn-in the basic form. A wall covered in white paper can be used for this purpose.

Using lines to work out the eye level on a photograph

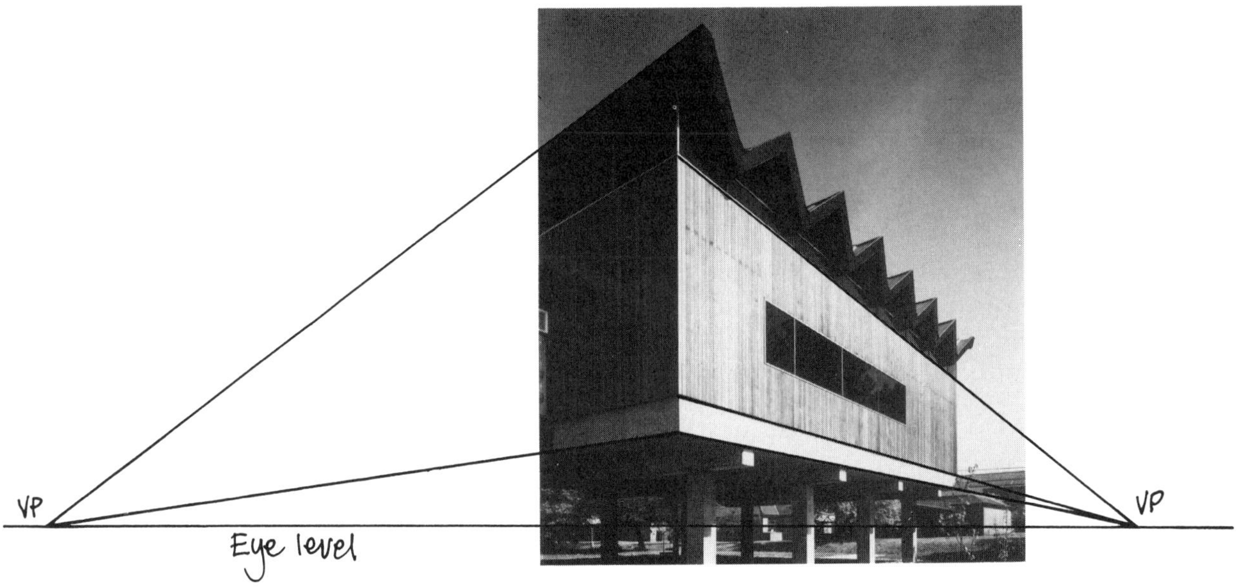

Assignment: *Find some photographs of objects or buildings. Cut them out and stick them on to a sheet of paper. Using the rules of perspective, work out where the vanishing points and the eye levels are.*

To draw in two point perspective, you must always start with the part of the object which is nearest to you. For instance, for a cube draw the *leading edge* first. Then from the top and bottom of this edge, draw feint lines to the two vanishing points.

Next, you must estimate the foreshortened depth of the object and draw in the back edges. Note that in two point perspective, all vertical lines are parallel.

From the top of the back edges, draw feint lines to the vanishing points. You can now draw-in the completed cube.

Estimating the depths of complex objects in perspective can be difficult by eye. On page 38 you will find a method to help you work them out more accurately.

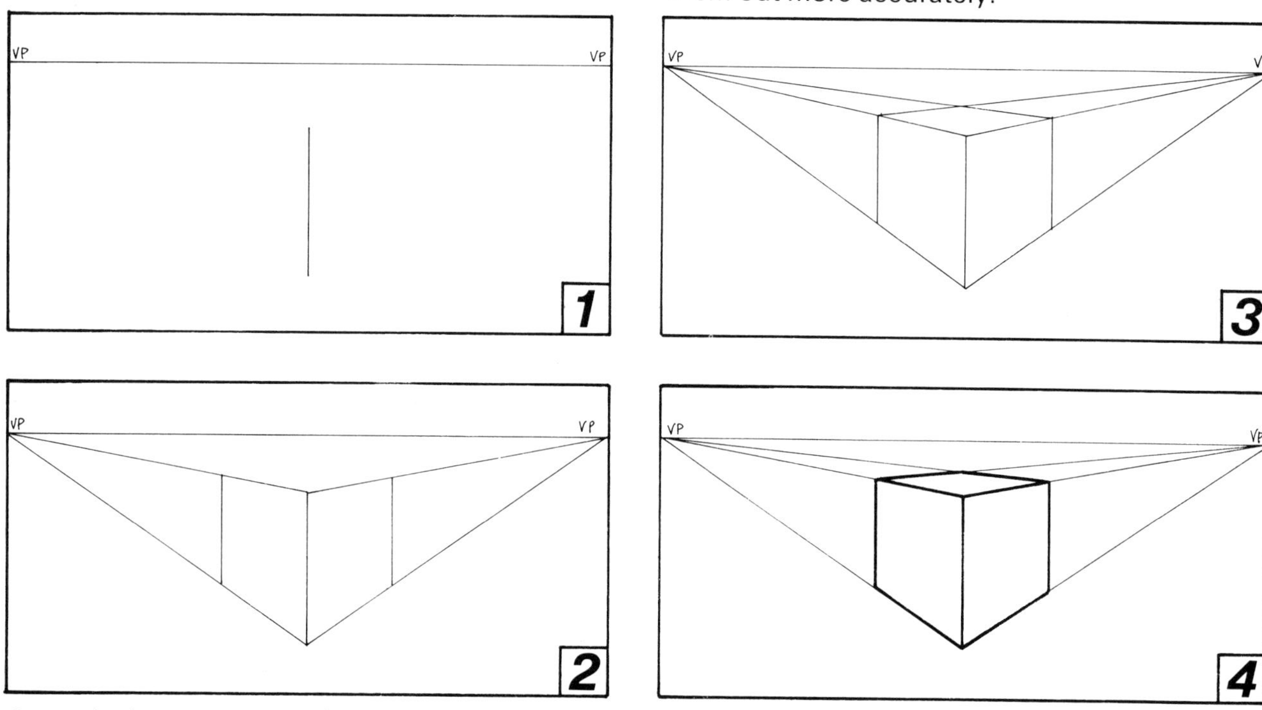

Stages in the construction of a two point perspective drawing

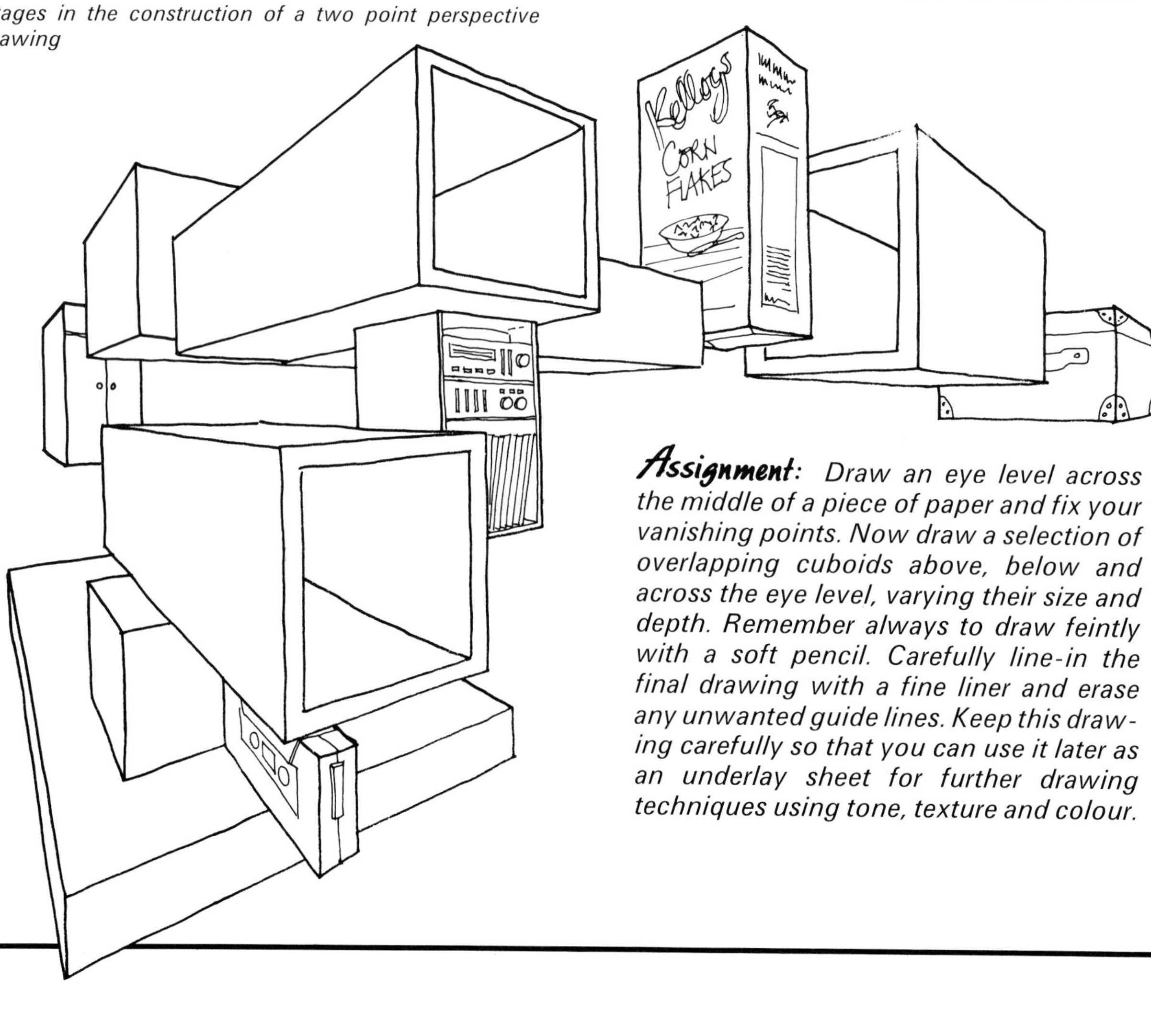

***Assignment**: Draw an eye level across the middle of a piece of paper and fix your vanishing points. Now draw a selection of overlapping cuboids above, below and across the eye level, varying their size and depth. Remember always to draw feintly with a soft pencil. Carefully line-in the final drawing with a fine liner and erase any unwanted guide lines. Keep this drawing carefully so that you can use it later as an underlay sheet for further drawing techniques using tone, texture and colour.*

▸ THREE POINT PERSPECTIVE

Three point perspective is seldom used, but can create some very interesting effects in a drawing. Here is how you can try three point perspective:

Draw an eye level at the top of your paper and then add three vanishing points. Two of the points should be on the eye level and the other should be positioned centrally at the bottom of the paper.

Start by drawing the front edge of the object and then continue as if you were drawing in two point perspective. With three point perspective, the only difference is that all the vertical lines now meet at the *third* vanishing point at the bottom of the page.

This effect can be used to distort scale and give the appearance of great height or depth, depending upon the position of the eye level.

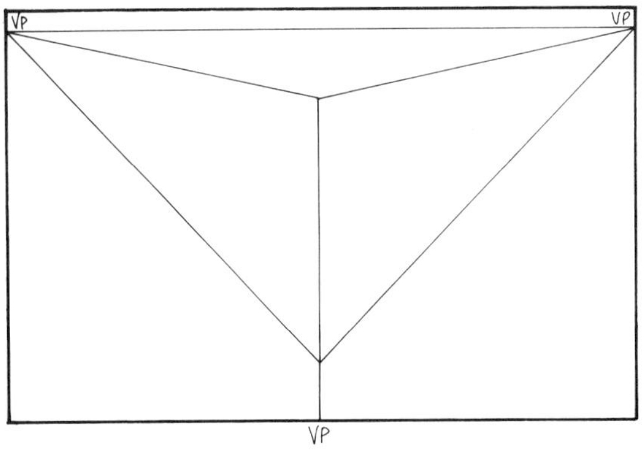

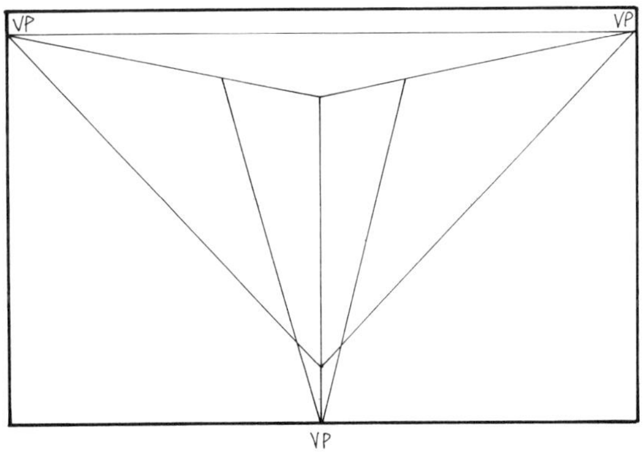

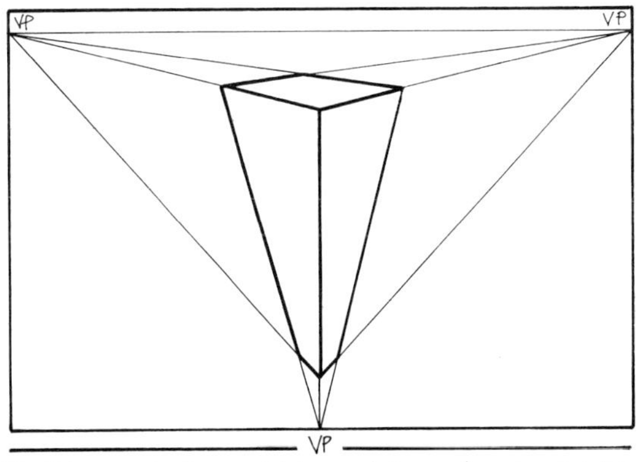

In this example the vanishing points are too close together, but this adds to the effect and creates a monumental look.

The photograph illustrates three point perspective

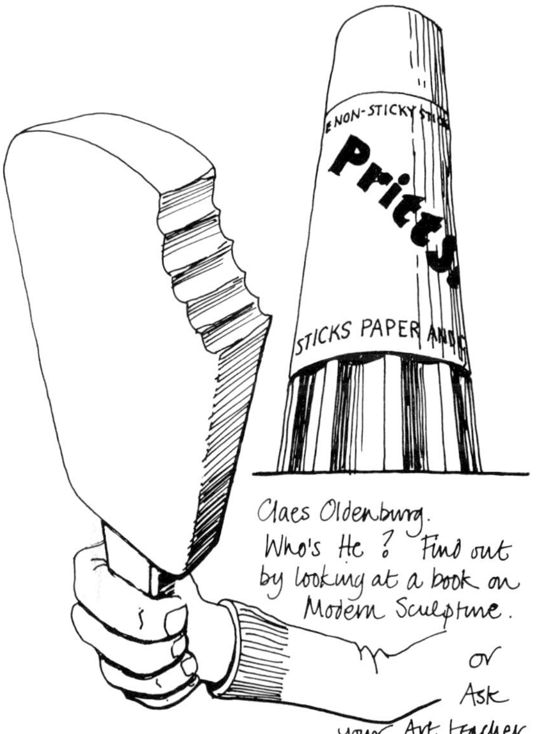

Assignment: *Take an everyday object, such as a cereal packet or personal stereo, and do a three point perspective drawing of it to make the object look monumental.*

▸ THE CIRCLE IN PERSPECTIVE

When a circle is drawn in perspective, it no longer looks like a circle! It becomes squashed by the effect of foreshortening into a shape called an **ellipse**. The ellipse will vary in width depending on how much of it is visible.

An ellipse has two axes: the **major axis** and the **minor axis**. Practise drawing different kinds of ellipse. Always start drawing from the minor axis so that you get good flowing curves at the edges. Draw several feint ellipses first, until you get the right shape, then line-in the best one.

Drawing ellipses

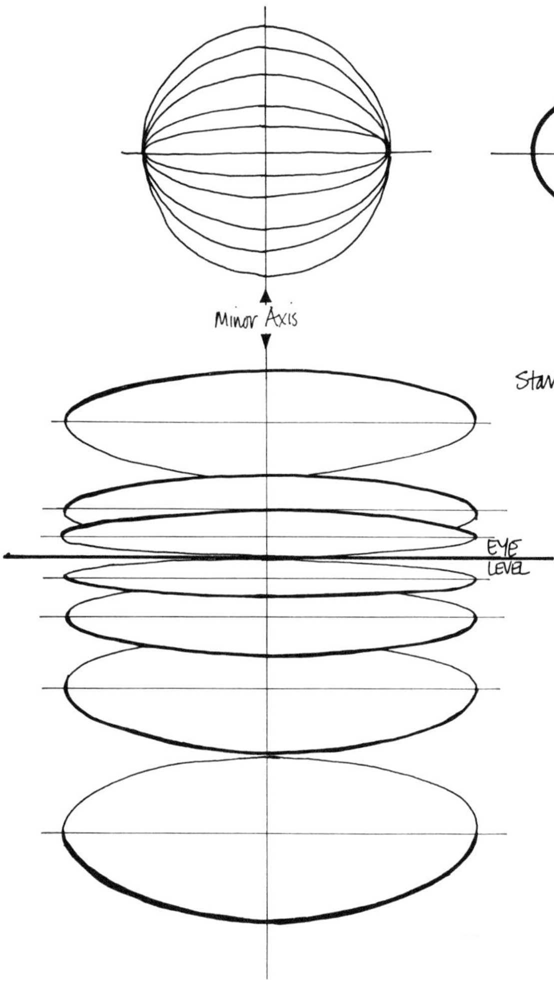

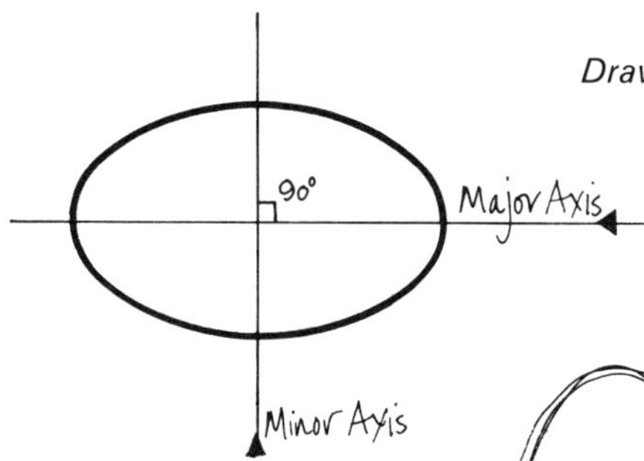

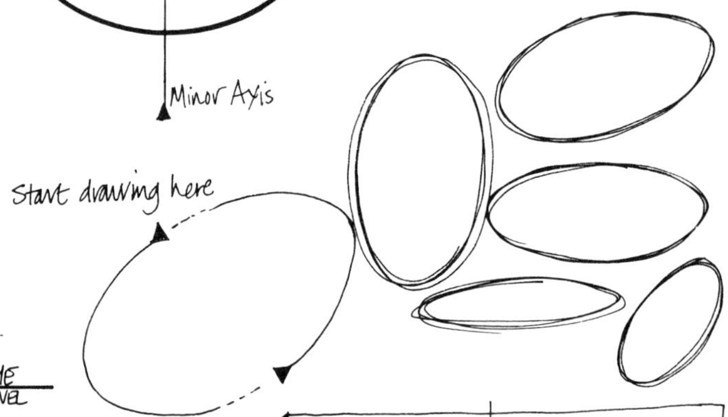

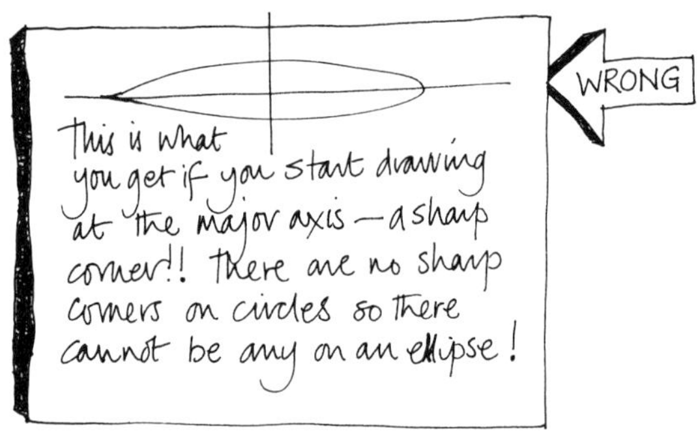

Ellipses around the home

▸ DRAWING CYLINDERS

When drawing a cylinder, it is useful to draw-in a feint centre line so that you can balance each half of the form.

For a vertical cylinder, draw the top ellipse first and then draw two vertical lines down from the edges of the ellipse. Decide on the length of the cylinder and then draw-in the base ellipse.

Always draw the whole of the ellipse—not just half of it. Remember that the further away from eye level the ellipse is, the more you will see of it.

Draw-in the ellipses so that their minor axes are in line to the vanishing point.

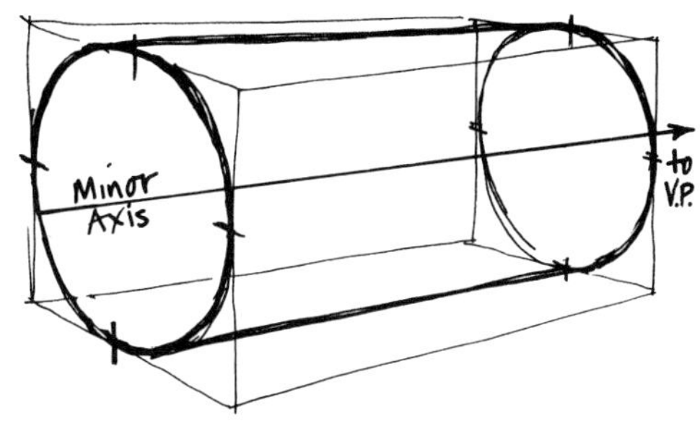

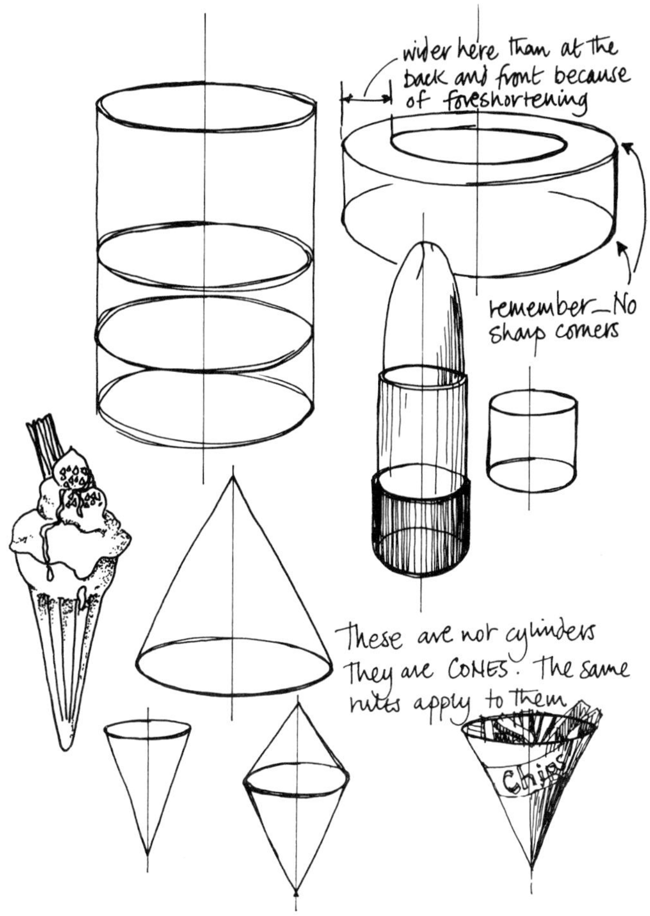

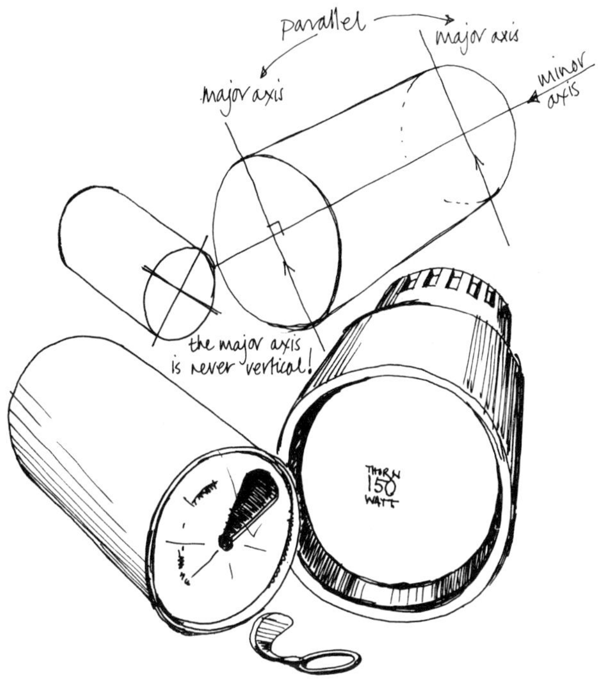

Two point perspective cylinders

To draw a cylinder in two point perspective, you must first draw a square cuboid in perspective and find the centre of each side of the square.

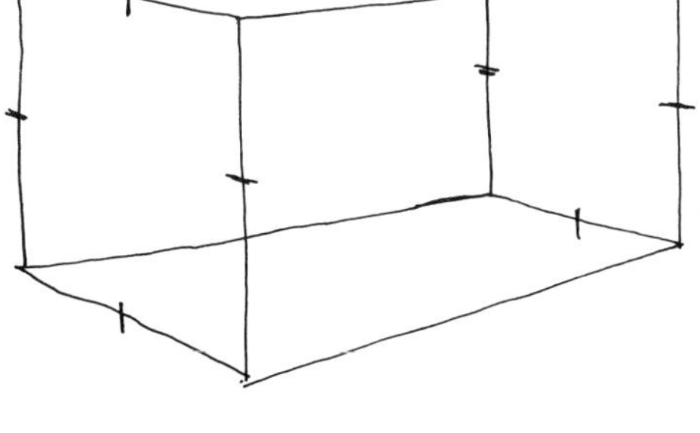

Assignment: *Find a selection of cylindrical forms of different sizes, such as a drinks can, a roll of adhesive tape, etc., and make careful drawings of them in both single and two point perspective. You could even try drawing the can in three point perspective to give it a monumental look. If the objects have labels on them, notice how they also follow the form.*

▸ STRENGTHENING LINE

To give more depth to your drawing, you can increase the strength of your lines. If you look into the distance, objects that are further away are not as clear as those nearest you. They also tend to look paler in colour. You can use this to good effect in your drawings. If you increase the strength of the lines closest to you and gradually decrease their strength as they recede (get further away), it will help to create more depth in your drawing.

You will probably have seen drawings where different thicknesses of line are used to emphasize parts and edges. This is a method used in line diagrams and drawings in **technical graphics**. It should not be confused with strengthening of line in freehand drawing.

***Assignment**: Practise drawing some forms using a strengthened line and then return to your drawing of overlapping cuboids. Use it as an underlay and produce the drawing using this technique.*

► COMPLEX FORMS

So far, you have looked at simple forms such as the cube and cylinder. Look around you, however, and you will see that most objects are not so simple! Fortunately, many man-made objects can be thought of as a number of basic forms, allowing us to draw them using a technique called **crating**. This is where the object is thought of as a number of smaller boxes (or *crates)*, each of which can be drawn in perspective.

It is sometimes useful to draw a side view of an object before crating. The side view can then be drawn on the crate and projected backwards to give the form.

If the object is cylindrical, such as a bottle, it is useful to draw a centre line so that you can balance each half. You may also need to use other forms, such as cones.

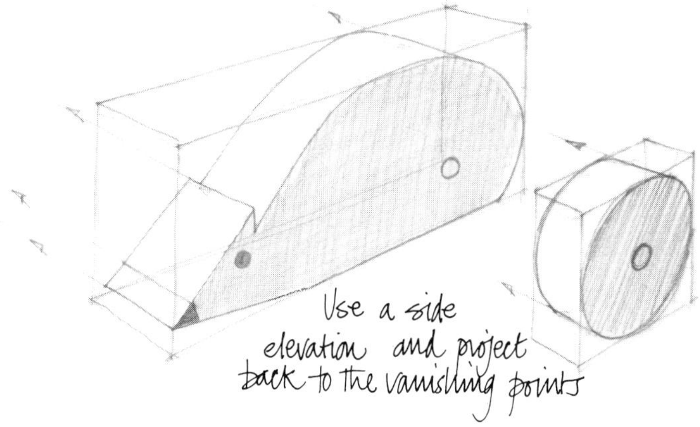

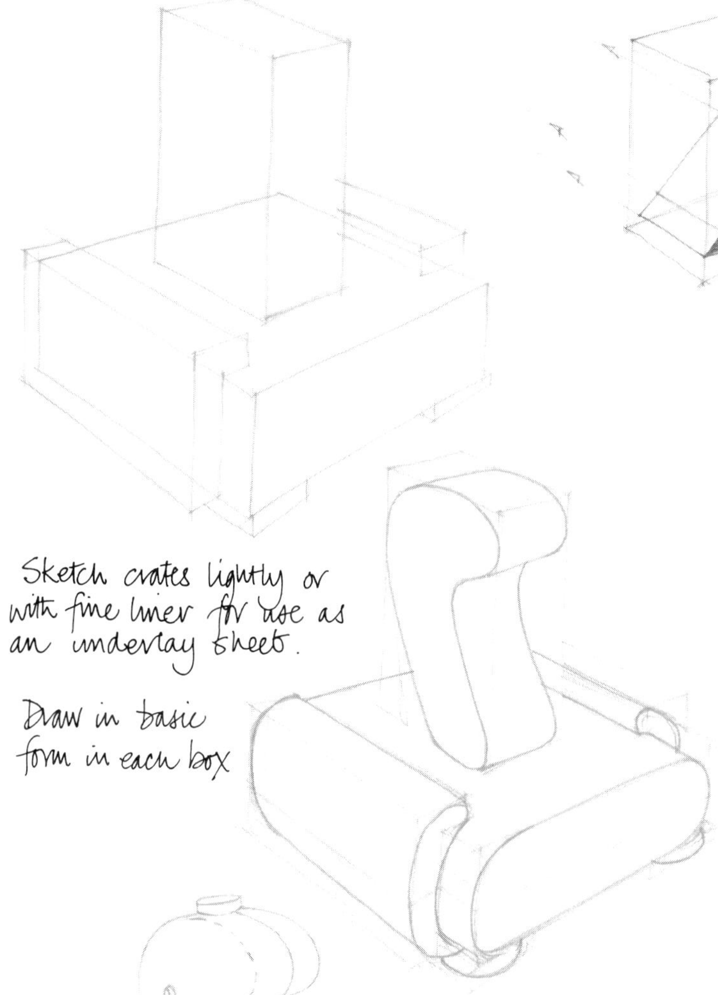

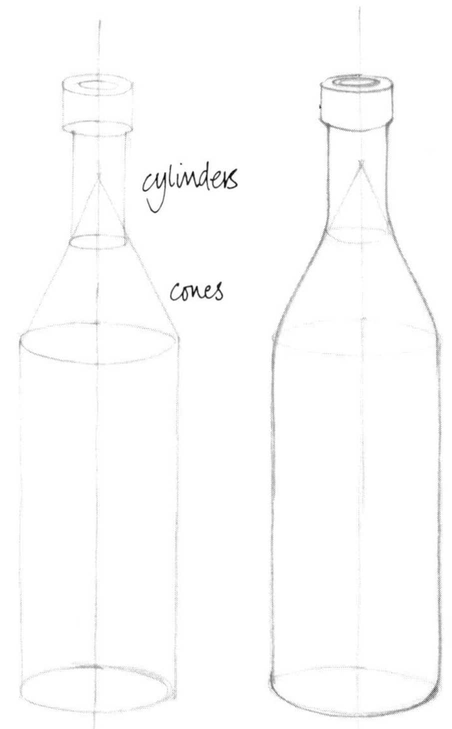

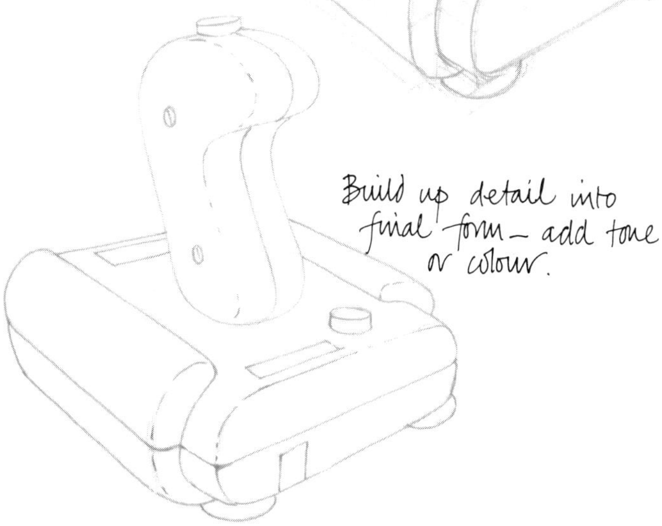

Assignment: *Find a number of more complex forms and make carefully-observed drawings of them using the crating technique. Remember to use a soft pencil and not to press too heavily.*

▸ ESTIMATING FORESHORTENING: THE CUBE METHOD

Sometimes there is a need to produce an accurate presentation drawing of a design in perspective. Crates, in the form of a number of cubes, can be used to estimate foreshortening more accurately.

Start by drawing one cube and draw-in the longest diagonals on the vertical sides.

Next, draw parallel lines to these diagonals from the lower back corner of the cube.

Repeat this until you have as many cubes as you need. If you need to build up the height, simply extend the diagonals and the vertical lines. Where they cross will be the top of the next row of cubes.

1

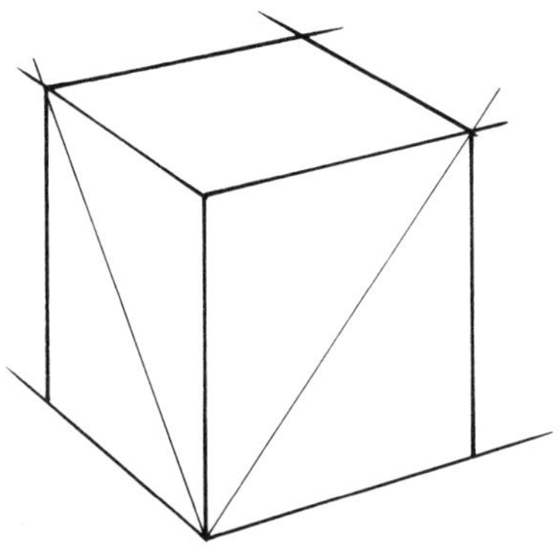

2

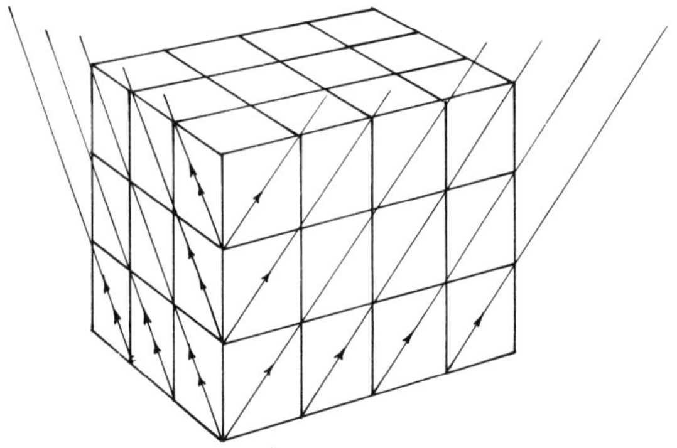

This builds up into a two-point perspective grid.

Assignment: *Using the cube method, make a carefully-observed drawing of a 13 amp plug, three times full size. Make a fine line drawing of the finished plug on an overlay sheet. This can then be further developed with tone or colour.*

Assignment: *Using a two point perspective grid, make a carefully-observed freehand drawing of an object such as a compact camera or torch. Use this as an underlay for a coloured rendering.*

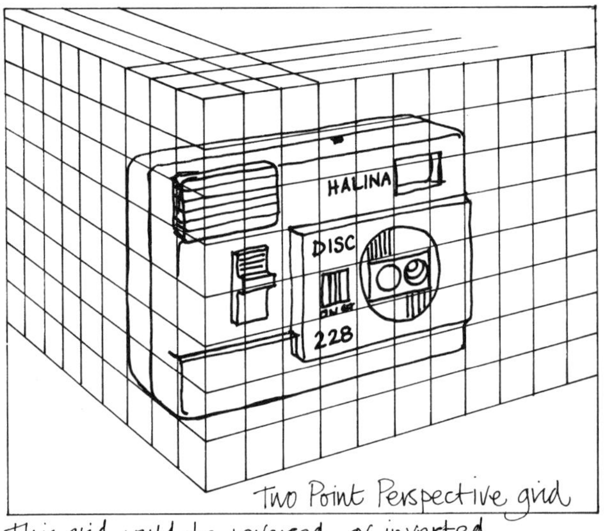

This grid could be reversed or inverted.

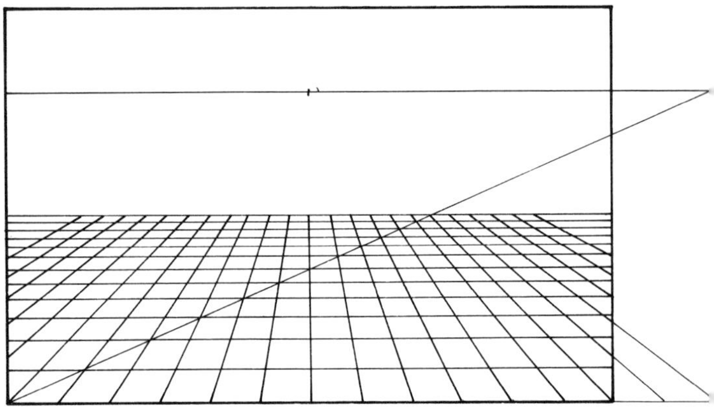

Single point perspective grids can also be used to estimate foreshortening

THE EFFECT OF LIGHT ON FORM

So far, you have used outlines to give the illusion of form to your drawings. When you look at real objects, however, you do not see lines around their edges. You only see the form because of the changes in **tone** or **shade** of the surfaces of the object. This change in tone is created by light. Why is this? What do you know about light rays?

Light casts shadows

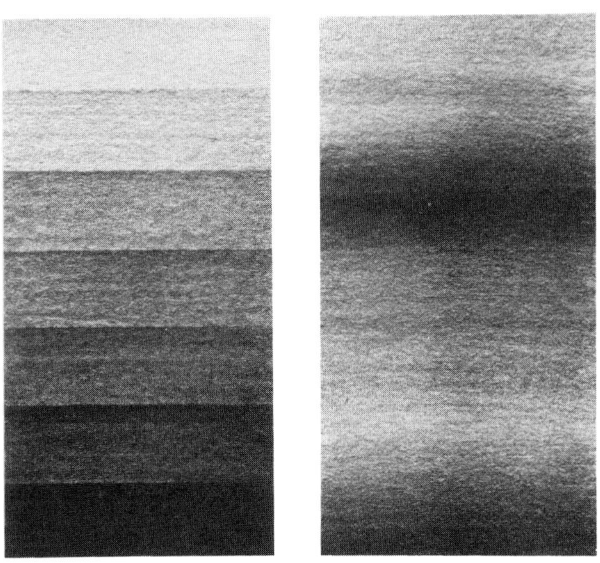

A range of tones produced by a 2B pencil

If you draw an object using a heavy outline and then add tone to the surfaces, it will look artificial; whereas if you sketch the outline *lightly* and add tone, the effect will be much more realistic.

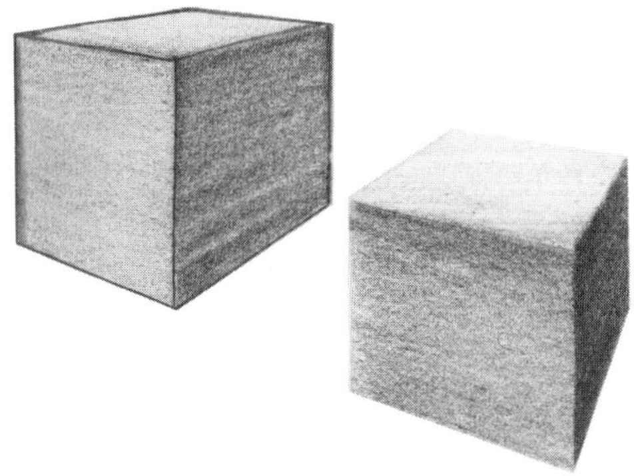

There are many sources of light: sunlight, electric light, the light from a candle, to name a few.

Can you think of any other sources of light?

When using tone, we first have to decide where the light is coming from. If there are many windows or lights in the room in which you are drawing, the tones on an object can become very confusing. It is therefore best to think of the light as coming from one source only. For the purposes of design drawings, it makes life easier to imagine the light coming over your left shoulder onto the object.

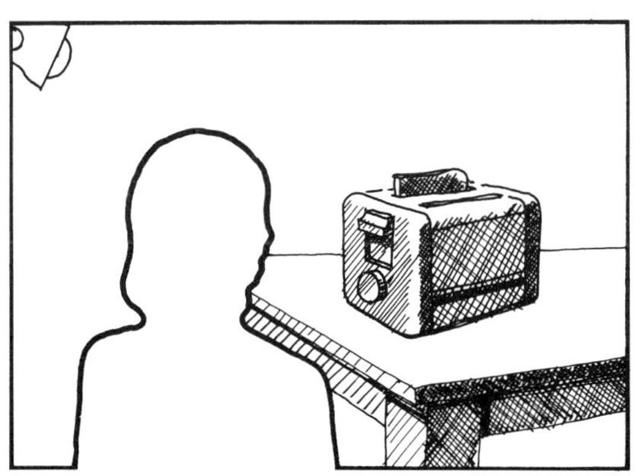

Imagine the light coming over your left shoulder

▸ ANGULAR FORMS

Look at the drawing of the cube below. All three sides are made up of slightly different tones. The top is the lightest and the side furthest from the light is the darkest. Notice that each tone covers the whole of the surface.

When adding tone or shading to a vertical surface, hold your pencil at a shallow angle so that more of the lead is in contact with the paper. Move your pencil backwards and forwards across the *whole area* to be shaded and move in the direction of the vanishing point. Do not stop in the middle of a surface as this will cause unevenness. It may help if you use a straight edge or a piece of scrap paper to protect the area you do not want to shade.

On a flat top-surface, the tone should be applied horizontally and faded slightly from front to back.

If the object is made from a shiny material such as plastic, the top surface may **reflect** some light. This can be shown by erasing some of the areas of tone on the surface. These areas should be parallel but not vertical. Do not overdo it—two or three areas will be enough.

Try shading a selection of angular forms, such as cuboids, prisms and pyramids.

Assignment: *Remember your drawing of the overlapping cuboids? Use the fine line drawing that you made as an underlay for a* ***tonal drawing*** *(drawing with tones added). Add the tone as though the light is coming over your left shoulder.*

▸ CURVED FORMS

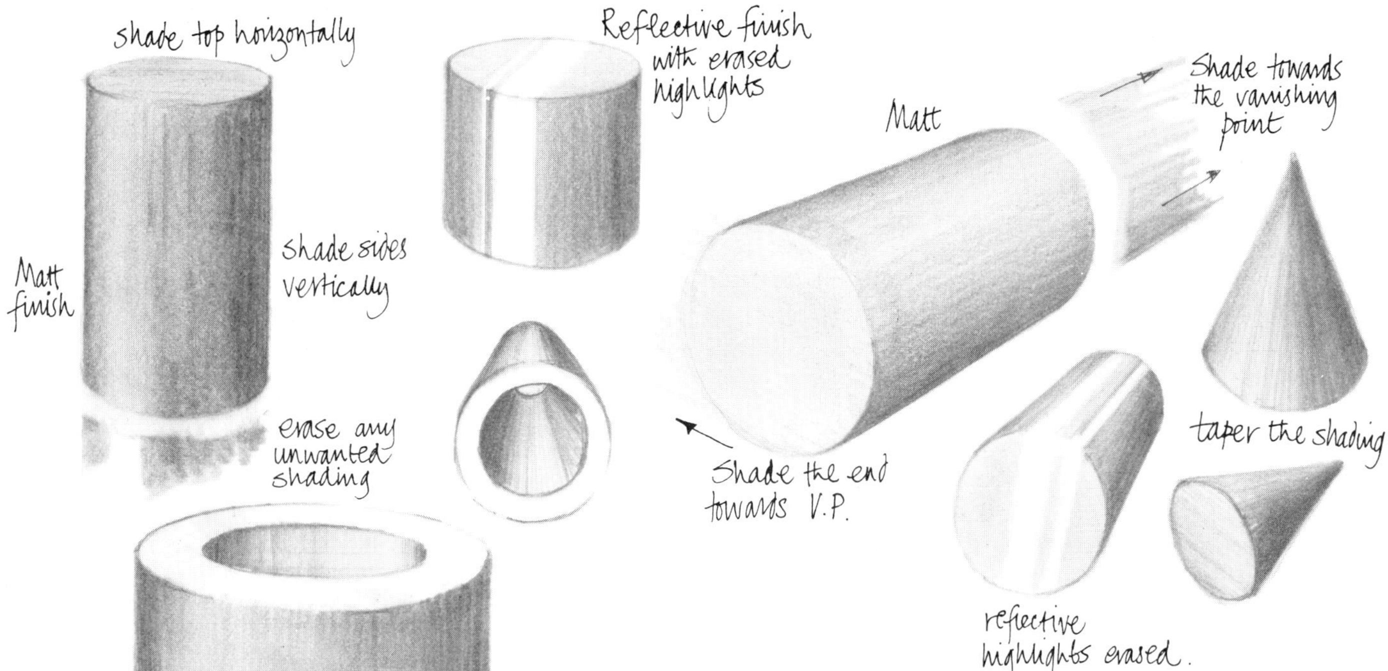

On a cylinder the tone will **blend** around the form. If the cylinder is in a standing position, the tone will run vertically.

If the cylinder is drawn in two point perspective, the tone will run towards the vanishing point. Any shading on the end of the cylinder will run towards its vanishing point.

Conical forms need to be shaded towards their **apex**.

***Assignment**: Use the drawings of the cans and the other cylindrical objects that you drew as an underlay to produce a tonal drawing.*

▸ SPHERICAL OBJECTS

A **ball** or **sphere** is different from any other form because it is completely curved. It is the only form that you can create from a flat shape: the circle.

You must think of it as having one highlight and from this point, the tone gradually becomes darker as you move round the form.

It takes quite a bit of practice to achieve this gradual shading.

▸ LINE SHADING

Lines can be used to create tone on the surface of forms. Look at the examples of line shading and notice the direction of the lines and the way they are spaced. Try using this technique on some of your drawings.

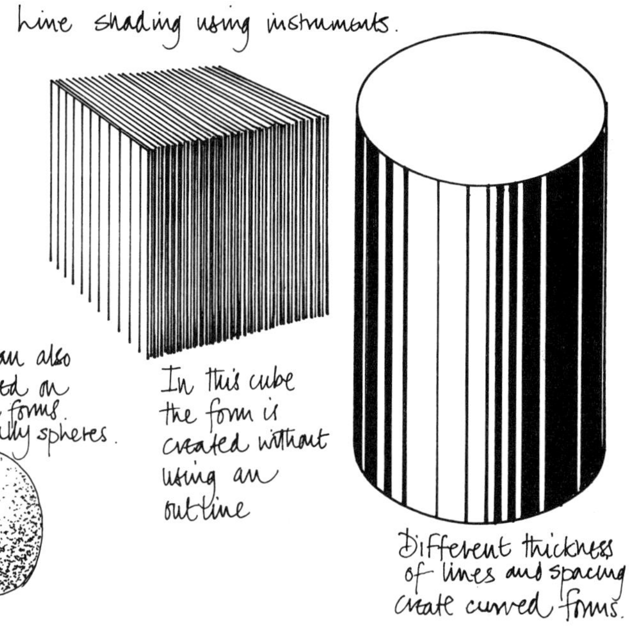

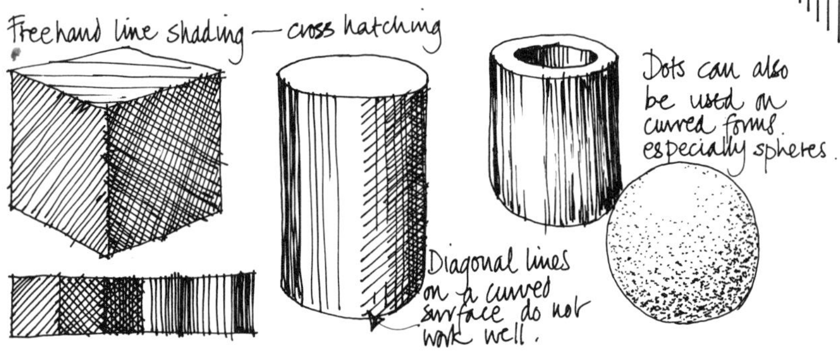

▸ LIGHT CASTS SHADOWS

If you draw and shade an object, but do not relate it to anything else, it will seem to 'float' on the paper.

To stop this 'floating', you can put the object on a surface. A surface can be suggested by simply drawing a straight line across the paper behind the object.

Once it is sitting on a surface, the object must cast a shadow onto that surface. The length and direction of the shadow depends upon the height and direction of the source of light: the higher the light, the shorter the shadow. The shadow can be constructed by drawing a line between the light, the top corners of the object and the surface on which it is sitting.

Observe carefully how shadows behave when one object is placed close to another. The shadow will follow the form of the object onto which it falls.

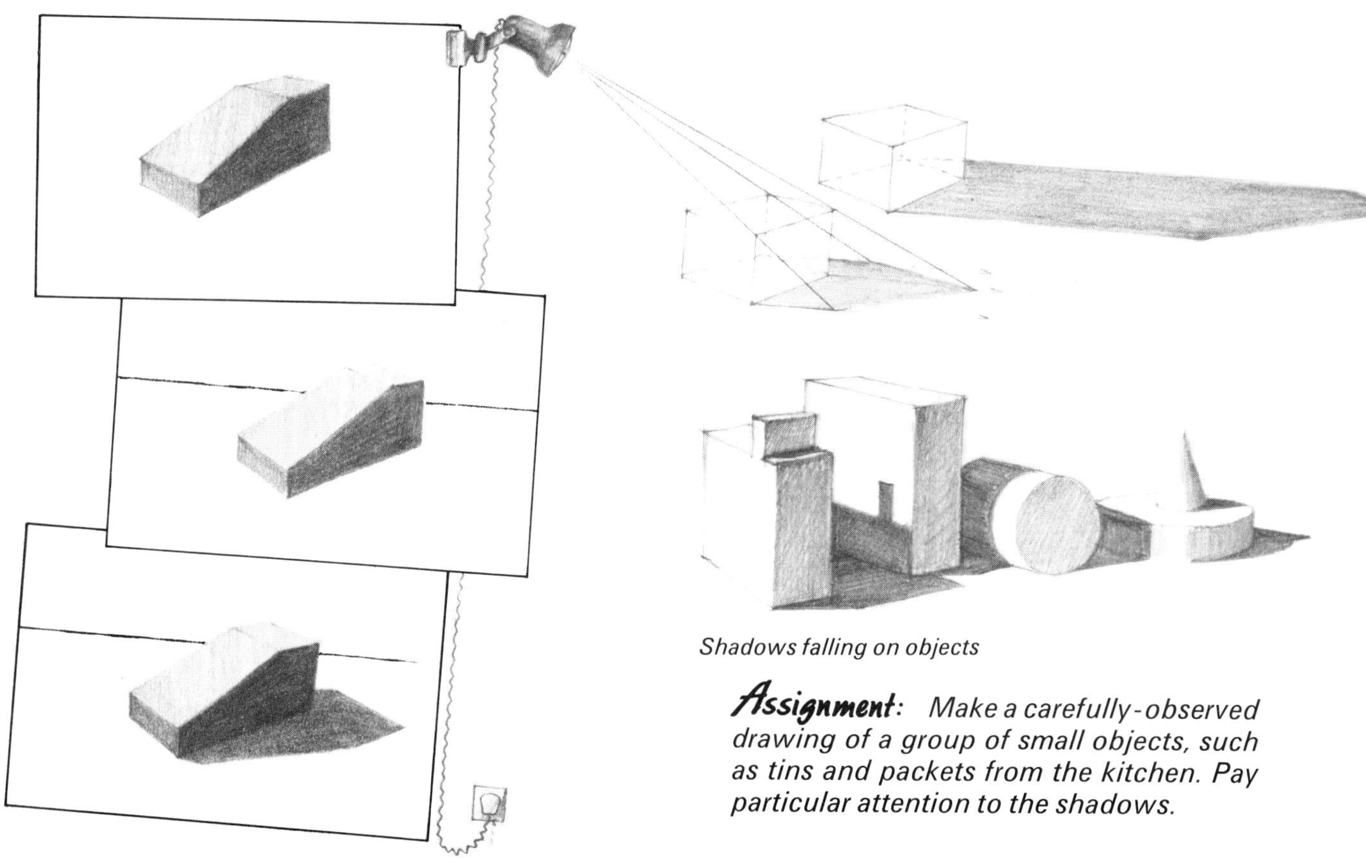

Shadows falling on objects

Assignment: *Make a carefully-observed drawing of a group of small objects, such as tins and packets from the kitchen. Pay particular attention to the shadows.*

Colour

The photograph shows a paper sculpture made from foldable card—a medium which can be used to good effect in design models

▸ USING COLOUR

Colour plays a very great part in our lives. The world would be a dull place without it! Natural colour is all around us in plants, animals, insects, rocks, etc. Many animals have developed colour as a **camouflage** so that they blend with their surroundings. Some use it so that predators find it difficult to see them; others use it so that they can surprise their prey.

Can you spot the hidden animal?

A warm colour scheme

A cool colour scheme

People have also developed the use of colour. Originally, they used natural **pigments** and **dyes**. These were obtained from such things as plants, earth and insects. Today, however, modern chemical substitutes are widely used to give an almost endless number of different **shades** and **tints**. Colours can also be referred to as **hues**.

We can communicate many ideas using colour. For example, we use sayings like 'red with rage', 'blue with cold' or 'green with envy'. In design, colour can be used to create 'moods' and colour schemes. Reds and oranges will give a 'warm' feeling whereas shades of blue will create a 'cool' mood. Red is often associated with danger in signs and symbols. Why do you think this is? Large firms, such as British Telecom, use colour as a means of identity.

DANGER

BhS

Colour used for identity

▸ MIXING COLOUR

There are three **primary colours** which cannot be achieved by mixing. These are red, yellow and blue. If you mix two 'primaries' together, you will create a **secondary colour**. There are three 'secondaries': orange, green and purple. Mixing two 'secondaries' will give a **tertiary colour**.

We quite often use a **colour wheel** to show the relationships of these colours to each other. The colour wheel was invented by Sir Isaac Newton in about 1666.

Black and white are known as **neutrals** and should not be called colours. They can, however, be mixed with colours to produce darker **tones** and paler **tints**. The variations possible are too numerous to name, but just looking at a colour chart will give you some idea of the selection available. Quite often, colours are known merely by numbers as in, for example, colour swatches, which most designers use.

Colour will greatly enhance your drawings and designs if it is applied carefully, but poorly applied colour will have the opposite effect.

▸ DESIGN SKETCHES

In design sketches, colour can be used to make shapes stand out from the background by **vignetting**. When doing this, take care to make the colour follow only one direction and do not simply echo the shape that you are vignetting.

Several drawings or design ideas can be linked together in a similar way, and it is not always necessary to go around the whole shape. The colour should not be too bright as this might detract from the shape or shapes that it surrounds.

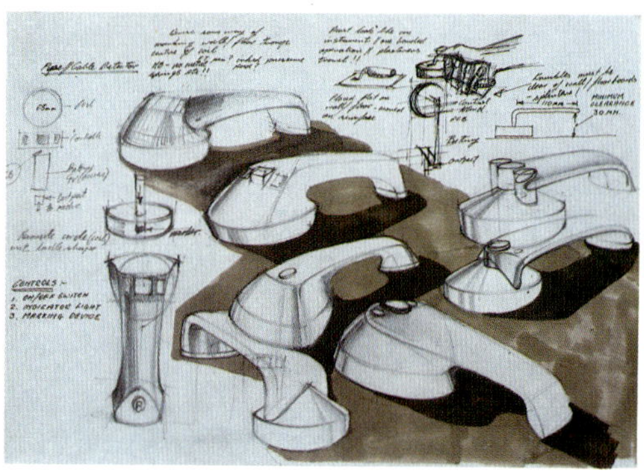

Neutral colour used to make design ideas stand out from the background

▸ PATTERN

Colour can also be used to great effect in pattern. Some colours will blend together well to give a subtle effect whilst others can be used to give vibrant exciting designs.

Colour pattern developed from observing a shell

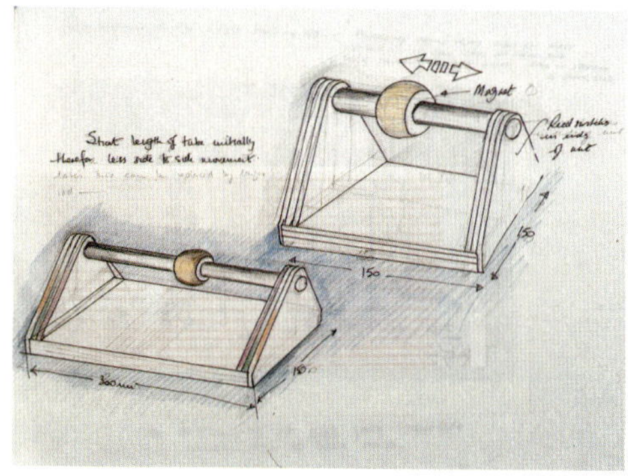

Subtle use of pencil crayon

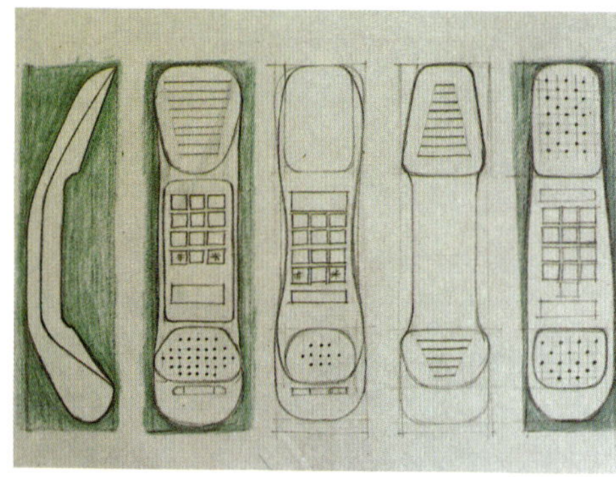

Colour used to isolate a chosen design

Above and below: Two examples of geometric patterns which use colour. What effect does each combination of colours have?

▸ EXPLODED VIEWS, SECTIONS AND DIAGRAMS

Colour can be used on exploded views, cross-sections and elevations to pick out different areas. It can also be used to emphasize parts or arrows in diagrams.

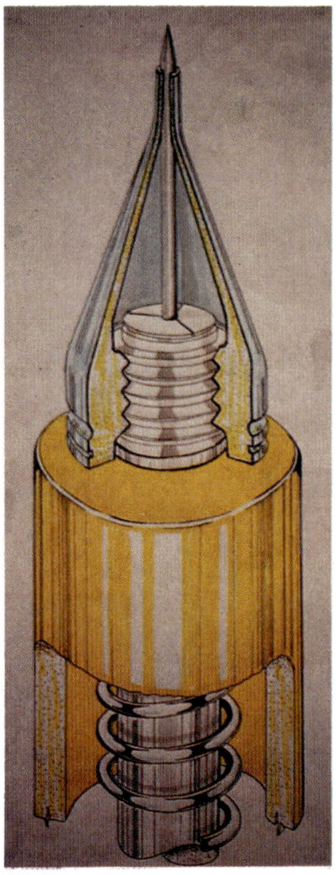

Cut-away view of a clutch pencil using markers on layout paper

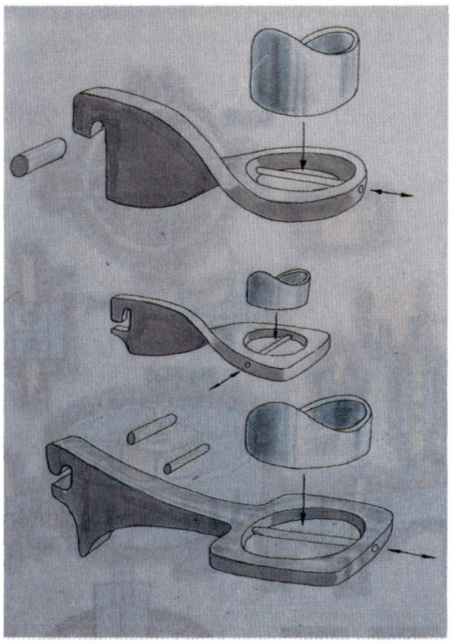

Exploded view using markers on layout paper. (Notice how layout paper allows you to see the drawing on the sheet below)

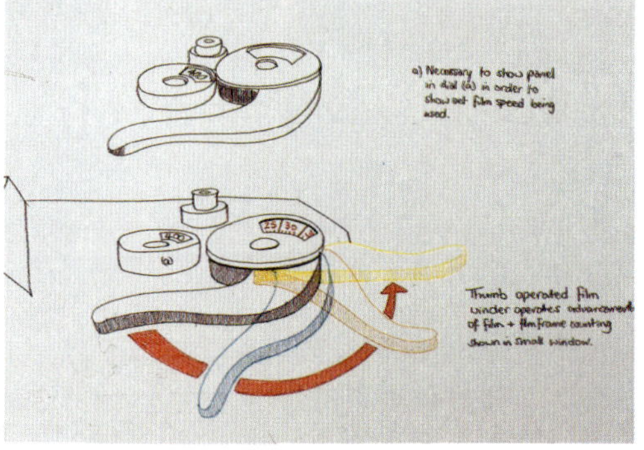

Sketch diagram showing a camera wind-on mechanism. The use of colour helps to emphasize the winder movements

▸ PRESENTATION

In presentation drawings, colour can be used to create a much more realistic image. It will improve the form and can also be used to suggest the material from which the object is made.

An airmarker has been used here to help create the impression of acrylic and gloss-painted wood

A pencil crayon has been used to simulate the painted metal of the artificial leg. A detail of one leg joint is enlarged and the yellow pointer indicates the position

PENCIL CRAYONS

Using a straight edge or finger nail to create straight or curved edges

Pencil crayons are available in a wide range of colours and are easy to use. They can be used in exactly the same way as drawing pencils and are easily erased as long as they have not been applied too heavily. Like drawing pencils, pencil crayons should always be kept sharp.

Different tones and effects can be created by using one colour over another. As a general rule, start with the lightest colour and darken up because it is almost impossible to use light colours over dark colours. Experiment with crayons to see what effects you can achieve.

When colouring an area, hold the pencil at a shallow angle to the surface. Work quickly across the whole area, varying the pressure if different tones are required. If you are working up to a straight line, use a ruler as a stop; if the edge is curved, use your finger nail to follow the line.

***Assignment**: Using a stencil cut from thin card, make a coloured pencil design of flat shapes which gives the impression of depth. Remember that colours seem to become paler as they recede (get further away). You may wish to use the overlapping technique in this piece of work.*

A white pencil crayon can be used to great effect to draw on black or dark-coloured paper. Try experimenting with coloured pencils on a variety of different papers to see what effects they create.

A stapler drawn with coloured pencils on sugar paper

Never simply 'fill-in' a pencil line drawing with colour. Black pencil lines around the edges of coloured surfaces make the drawing look artificial. Instead, either use the line drawing as an underlay sheet, or use the pencil crayon itself to lightly draw the outlines.

When adding colour to perspective drawings, you must consider the angle and strength of light on the object. Shadows on coloured objects are never grey or black: they are always

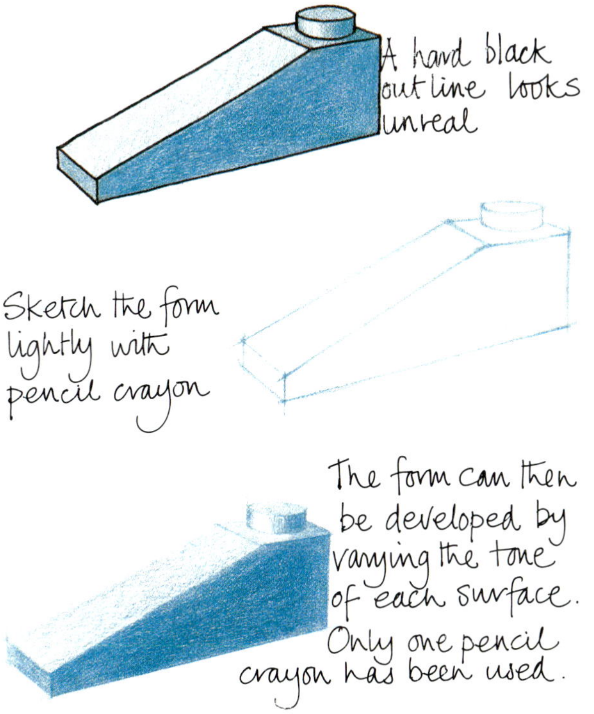

An electric jug kettle drawn with coloured pencils on brown wrapping paper

darker tones of the surface colour of the object. As with a pencil shading, you should imagine that the light is coming over your left shoulder.

***Assignment**: Try adding colour to a selection of geometrical forms using just one crayon at first. Then experiment by making drawings using two or more crayons to create darker tones. Make notes on which colours you used for each drawing so that you have a reference for future work.*

Colour can be used to create the effect of different materials. Close observation of materials is very important if you are to draw them realistically.

For example, wood can be drawn realistically by looking carefully at the **grain patterns** and colours.

Shiny surfaces can be suggested by the use of **highlights**. Highlights can be created by either leaving the paper white in places, or by erasing areas of crayon after colouring.

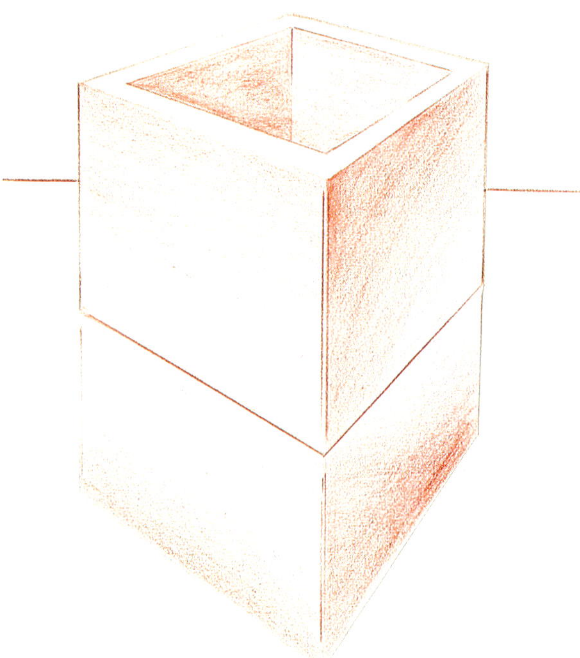

Cube on a reflective surface

Assignment: *Find four simple objects which are made of different materials and have different surface qualities. Make careful coloured pencil drawings of them. Note down how you achieved the various effects for future reference.*

Chrome or polished metal will have strong **reflections** on its surface. A chrome object is often drawn as though it is sitting in the middle of a desert under a blue sky. The sand is reflected on the lower parts of the object and the sky on the top surface.

Do not confuse reflections with shadows. What is the difference?

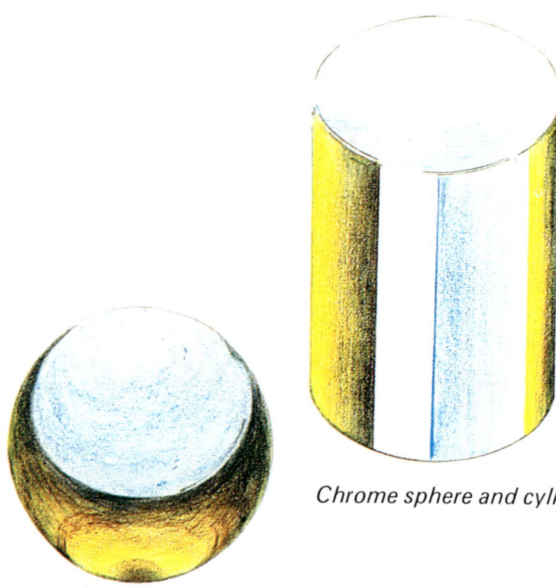

Chrome sphere and cylinder

Assignment: *You will remember that when an object is placed on a surface or against another object, it casts a shadow. This shadow will be a darker tone of the surface onto which it is cast. It will not be grey or black unless the background is neutral. Make a drawing of a group of simple objects to observe how their shadows and reflections affect each other.*

PASTELS

Chalk pastels are very versatile and can be used in a variety of ways for drawing lines and areas. They are especially useful for suggesting the top surfaces of objects made from plastic.

They can be blended together easily and may be erased to create highlights. Once a chalk pastel drawing has been completed, it must be sprayed with a **fixative** to stop it smudging.

To achieve a large, even area of colour, the 'cotton wool technique' can be used:

> Scrape a small amount of pastel on to a separate piece of paper. If you wish to mix colours, you can do it at this stage by blending the powdered pastel.
> Using clean cotton wool dabbed into the powdered pastel, apply even strokes of colour diagonally across the surface. Don't worry about going over the edge of the shape you want to be coloured, as this can easily be erased later.
> Using an eraser, rub-in any highlights you want to show.
> **NB**: Once the pastel has been fixed it cannot be erased.

Areas of pastel colour applied in this way can be built up further by coloured crayon or marker. Practise the technique on some simple forms.

1 Scrape off a small amount of pastel

3 Rub-in any highlights that are to appear

2 Apply even strokes of colour across the surface

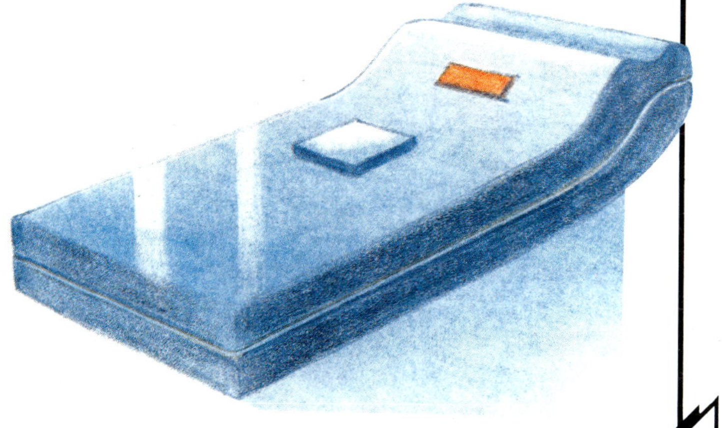

A fuse tester drawn with pastel

MARKERS

There are hundreds of different kinds of marker available at present, and new ones are constantly being produced. They can be divided into two main types: **water-based** and **spirit-based**. They also come with a number of tip shapes: **fine line, bullet, wedge** or **chisel**.

Fine line, bullet and wedge marker tips

▸ WATER-BASED MARKERS

These come in a rather limited range of colours, making subtle shading difficult. They also tend to have very hard tips, which can cause the surface of the paper to 'scrub up' giving uneven areas of colour.

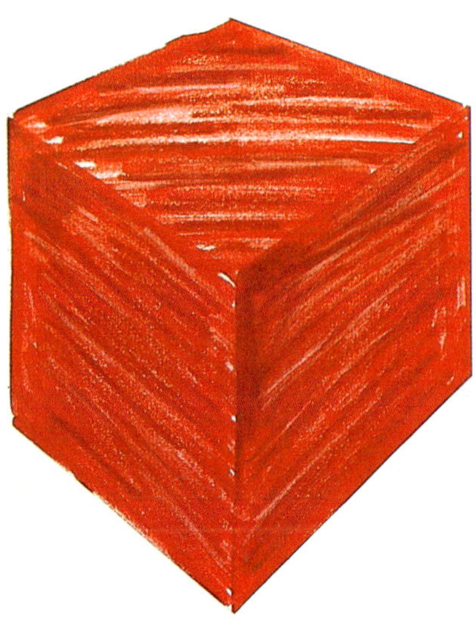

Uneven areas of colour tend to distort the surface of the form.

▸ SPIRIT-BASED MARKERS

These usually come in a much wider colour range and are often used by professional designers. They give a smooth, even flow of colour which dries quickly and does not affect the stability of the paper.

Special **bleedproof papers** are produced but these are not essential. If you are *not* using a bleedproof paper, always put another sheet of paper under your drawing in case the marker ink does 'bleed' through. This is especially important if you are using a plastic drawing surface because the marker spirit may act as a solvent and eat into the plastic if it reaches it.

Try out some spirit-based markers on a variety of papers. Always remember to replace the top of the marker immediately after use, to prevent it drying out, and always work in a well ventilated area.

Spirit markers used on different papers

NB: Although spirit-based markers are **permanent** when applied to paper, they are not **light fast**. In other words they will fade if left in sunlight.

▸ USING SPIRIT-BASED MARKERS

These markers will draw three thicknesses of line.

Practise all of them. Make sure you are holding the marker in the correct position for each line width. Check this on a scrap piece of paper before you start.

Don't be frightened—make quick strokes. The longer you leave the tip on the paper, the more ink will be drawn out. Going over an area two or even three times will darken the shade.

To fill an area, you can work freehand to a line or you can **mask** the area with tape, paper or film. If you want a flat area of colour, work quickly keeping a wet tip edge as you move across the surface. You can, however, also put the marker's **streaking** effect to good use to give direction to a surface.

Practise rendering geometrical forms with markers in a variety of ways. Try to create different surface finishes. Also, you can try using coloured papers or brown craft paper.

Markers can be supplemented with pencil crayons, which can be used to add fine detail. A white crayon is especially useful for highlights. Highlights can also be applied using gouache or liquid paper.

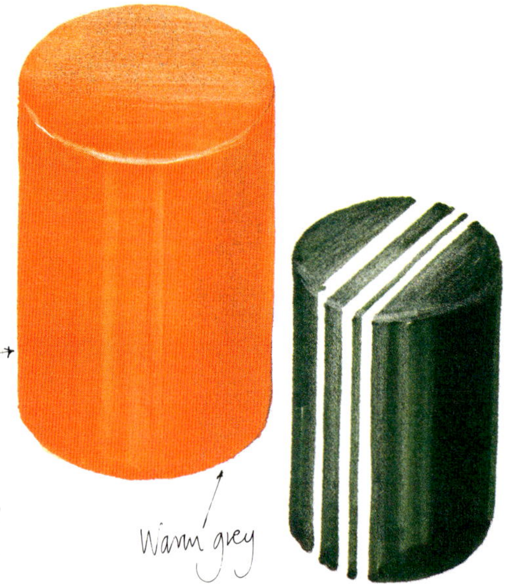

Assignment: *Look carefully at the rendering of the radio-cassette. See how the marker has been used to create the impression of shiny plastic? Make an orthographic line drawing of a small, colourful plastic object, such as a compact camera, personal stereo or radio. Render the drawing using markers. Don't worry if you go over the edge of the shape, you can cut the drawing out using a scalpel and mount it on another sheet. Use pencil crayons to build up details on top of the marker.*

ADDING COLOUR BY SPRAY

There are a number of ways of **spraying** colour on to a surface, each of which will give a different effect. Whichever method you use, you will have to mask off the surrounding area in some way. Methods of masking are shown on page 59. Try to work on a horizontal surface to minimize the risk of the colour running.

▸ METHODS OF SPRAYING

Splatter is a coarse, random effect created when you dip an old toothbrush into paint or ink and then scrape a piece of stiff card across the bristles.

Splatter with a toothbrush

A **diffuser** will also give a fairly coarse area of colour. To use a diffuser, you dip one tube into the paint or ink and then blow down the other one. Air rushing over the top of the first tube causes the paint or ink to be drawn up. It is then sprayed out on to the surface. With practice, you can control the spray but don't try to blow too hard!

NB: always wash out the diffuser after use.

Spraying with a diffuser

Both the splatter and the diffuser can be used to cover larger background areas on to which other renderings can be mounted. The backgrounds to be sprayed can either be masked off before spraying or cut out and pasted into position after spraying.

Airbrushed rendering of a telephone mounted on a splatter background

The photograph of the car is mounted on a background which has been partly created by a diffuser

***Assignment**: Find a colour photograph of an object such as a car in a brochure or magazine and cut it out. Combine it with a number of different background areas and shapes using the splatter or diffuser methods. Think carefully about which colour and shape will show the photograph off to best effect. Finally, glue the background and photograph into place on a larger sheet.*

The Letraset Airmaker is a relatively new development for spraying medium-sized, finished presentation drawings and models. It consists of a small plastic holder which is connected to a compressed air supply and into which is fitted a **Pantone fine marker**. When the valve is pressed, compressed air is forced through the tip of the pen, causing the ink to be sprayed out. Colour can be changed instantly by simply swopping pens. These pens are spirit-based, so remember to replace the caps immediately after use.

It takes practice to get an even area of colour using the airmarker. Start by masking-up some basic shapes either using tape or a cut-out paper stencil. Spray evenly back and forth across the area *always starting and finishing outside the shape.* Start from about 150 mm away and work your way in closer, if necessary.

Gradually build up the colour to the required intensity. Don't be frightened of building up to a slightly darker tone than you think you need. When you remove the masking, the area you have sprayed will almost always appear lighter. Always start with the *lightest* colour first. It is almost impossible to apply light colours over darker ones.

Work slowly across the area

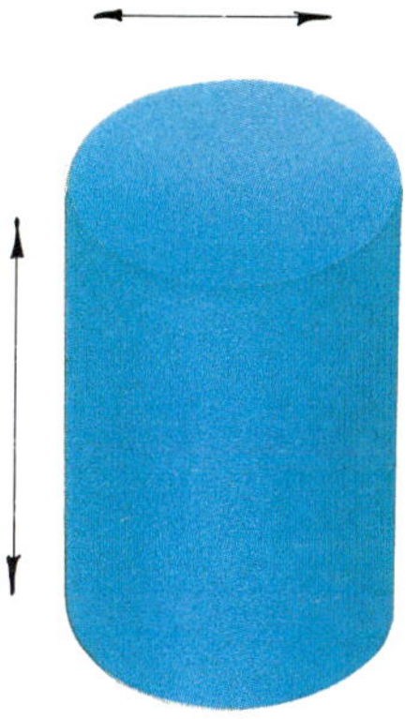

Spray the cylinder in the direction of the arrows

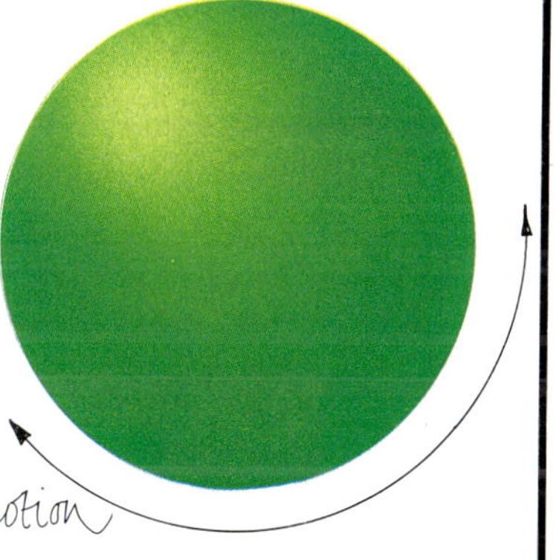

To render a sphere you must work around the form in a circular motion

This rendering of the Airmarker was produced by using an Airmarker. The highlights have been added later with white pencil crayon.

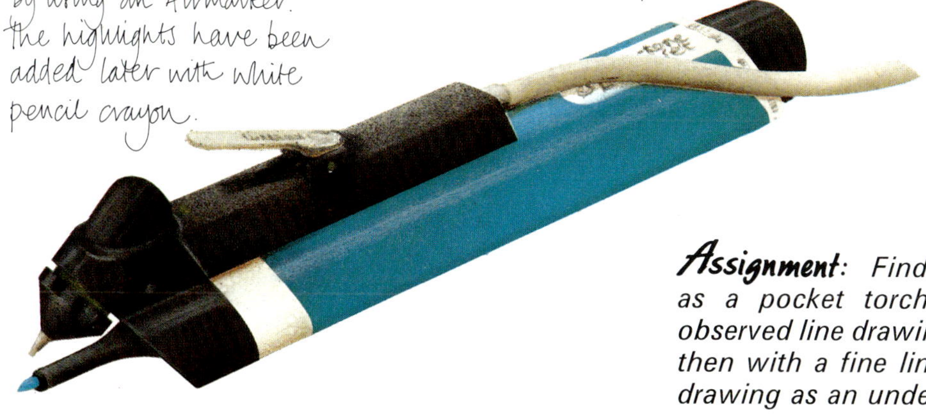

***Assignment**: Find a small object such as a pocket torch. Make a carefully-observed line drawing firstly in pencil and then with a fine liner. Use the fine liner drawing as an underlay sheet and render the drawing using a variety of media, including an airmarker. Mount these renderings on different backgrounds.*

The photographs below all show examples of packaging and modelling, dealt with in the following pages

Clown pop-up greetings card (p. 64)

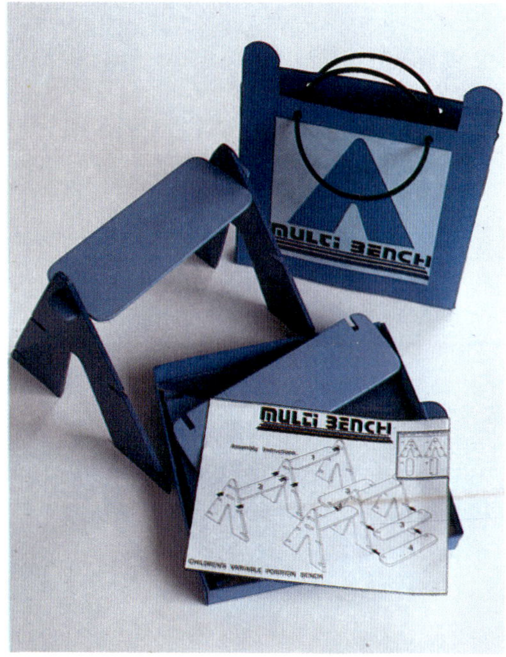

Scale model, packaging and instruction sheet for knock-down bench units

Accurate visual model made from jellutong (p. 73)

Development of a Yorkie Easter egg box (p. 66)

Blister packaging and point-of-sale display for small electrical goods (p. 77)

Aerosol sprays can be used for large areas and will give an even covering of colour. Always build up the colour in thin layers when using an aerosol spray. Make sure that you spray in a *well ventilated place,* especially if using cellulose-based paint. Mask off the surrounding area well.

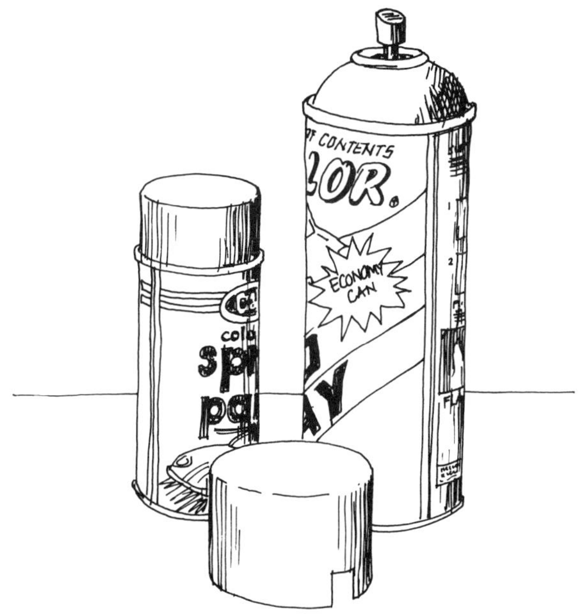

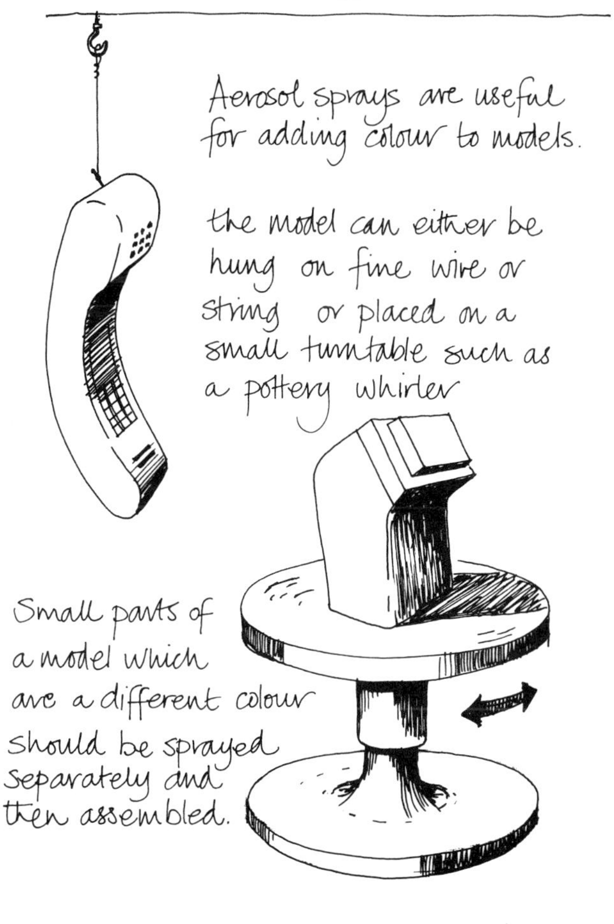

▸ MASKING FOR SPRAYING

Masking areas for spraying can be achieved using **tape**, **paper stencils** or special **low-tac masking film**.

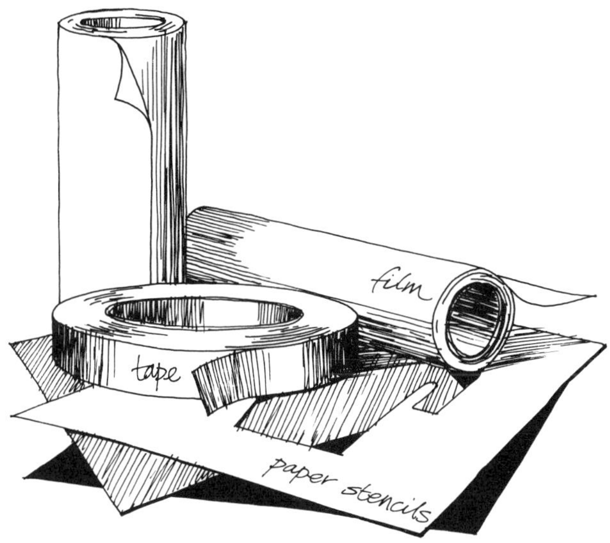

Masking tape gives a good straight edge to an area which is to be sprayed, and can be used with paper. Make sure you test the paper surface first: use a scrap piece of paper to see that the tape can be removed without damaging the surface. If necessary, some of the 'tac' can be removed from masking tape by sticking it to a plastic surface and peeling it off again. It is then ready for use on the paper surface.

Large areas can be masked with newspaper and tape. Interesting effects can be achieved by tearing the paper and using without tape.

When using an airmarker or airbrush, you will need to produce a **stencil** for the areas to be coloured. For a simple object, a **tracing paper stencil** will be sufficient. A more complex and detailed rendering will require the use of masking film.

▸ TRACING PAPER STENCIL

To make a tracing paper stencil, you must first trace the original line drawing, paying special attention to the lines where a colour change takes place.

Taking a scalpel, carefully cut along all the lines of the stencil, keeping all the pieces you cut out. Do this on a **cutting board** or **mat**, not on a drawing board or table top!

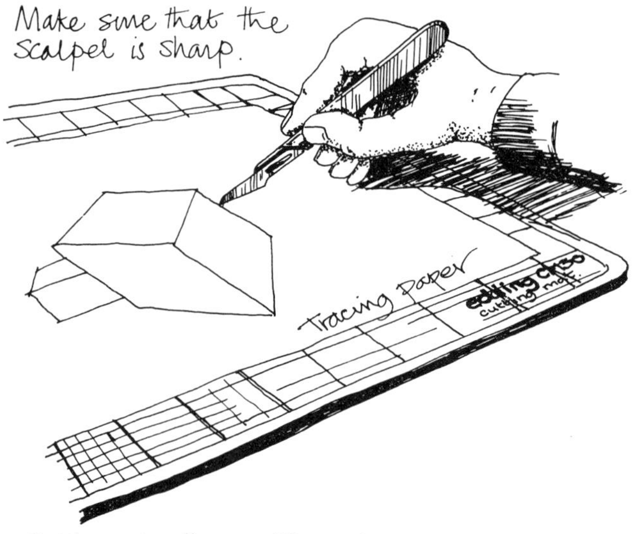

Cutting a stencil on a cutting mat

Reassemble all the pieces on the surface of your paper. Then decide which areas are to be the palest and remove the corresponding parts of the stencil. Weight the remaining parts of the stencil down with small objects. Don't use pins—they will leave unsightly holes in the paper.

Spray the area until the required intensity is achieved. Repeat the process for each area of the rendering, leaving the darkest until last.

Spraying through the stencil

A photocopy of the drawing can be used as an alternative to a tracing paper stencil, and another way of keeping the paper stencil in place is to work over a magnetic surface (such as a sheet of tinplate) and use small magnets instead of weights.

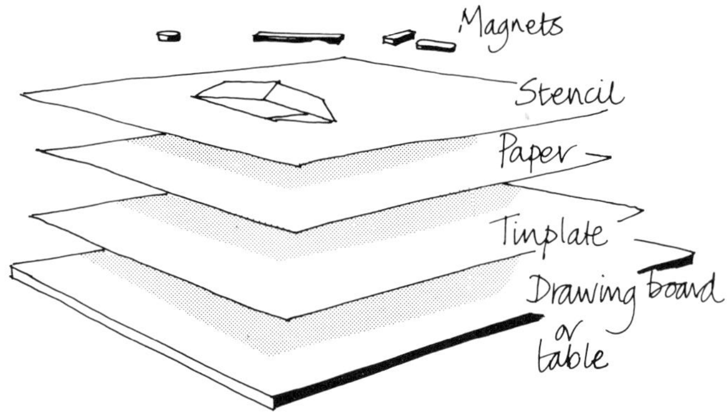

▸ MASKING FILM

Masking film is a low-tac self-adhesive film of plastic on a supportive paper backing. The paper backing is removed and the film is placed over the drawing to be rendered. A scalpel is then used to cut carefully through the film. Areas can then be removed for spraying.

It takes a lot of practice to be able to cut through the film without cutting the drawing as well. Always keep *all* the areas of film so that they can be replaced when you are spraying the different-coloured areas.

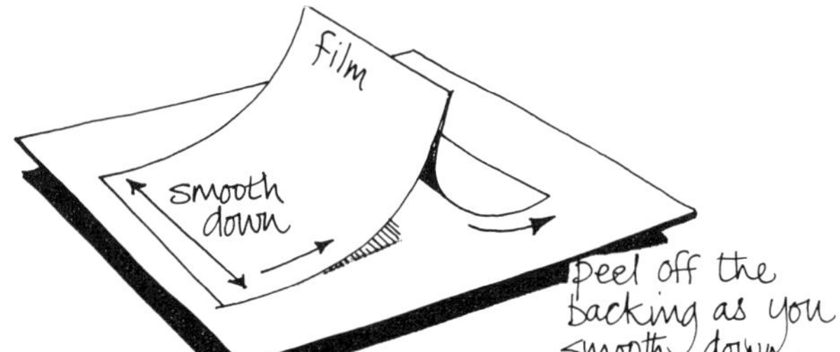

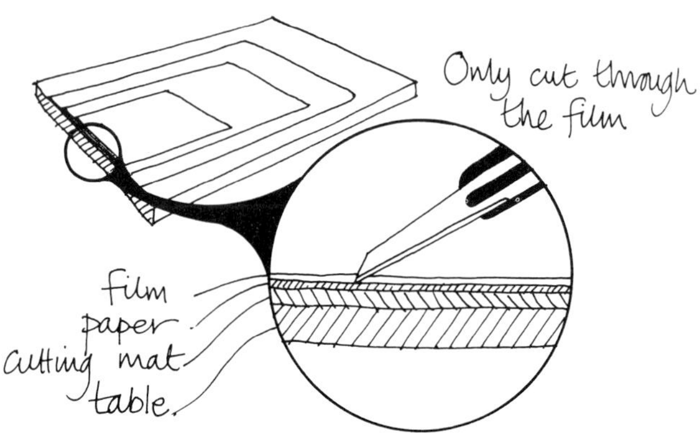

EXPLODED DRAWINGS

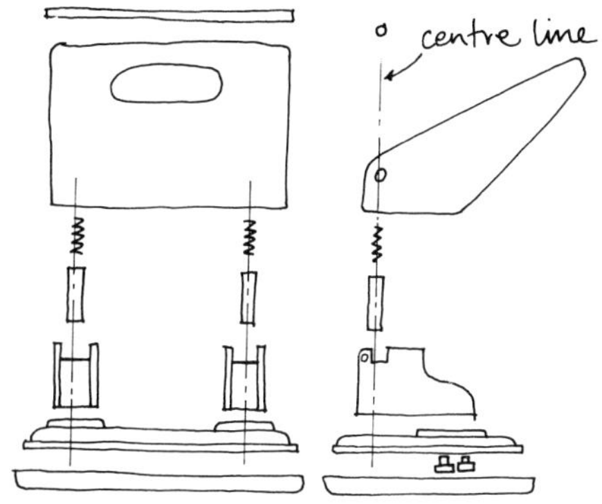

If something explodes, it breaks up into smaller, separate parts. An **exploded drawing** shows all the parts of an object separately, but in proper relation to each other. Exploded drawings are mainly used to give information in manuals or in assembly instructions.

Before you attempt the three-dimensional exploded view, it is important to record carefully how each piece of the object that you are drawing fits together. Draw a sketch elevation for this purpose. When drawing the exploded view, use construction and centre lines to ensure that all the separate parts line up.

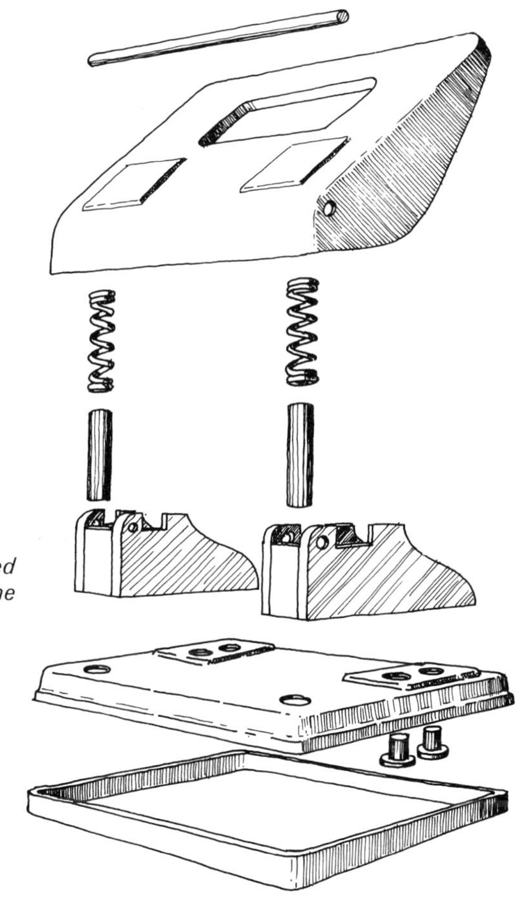

Orthographic and perspective exploded views of a paper punch and (below) the complete punch

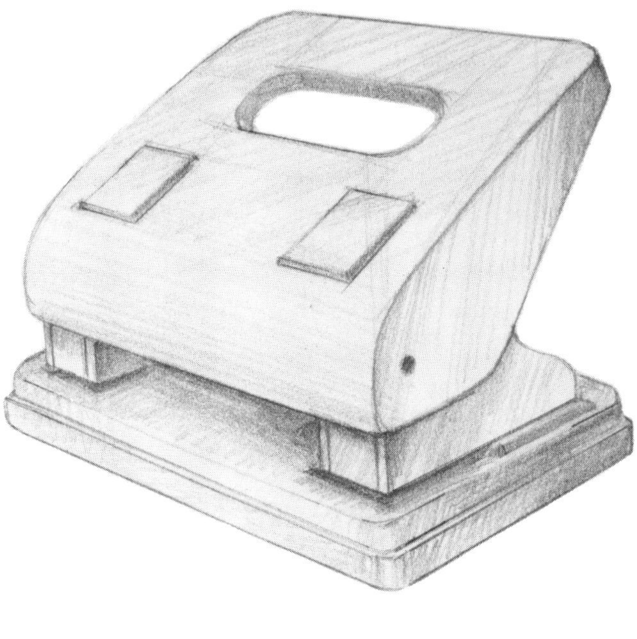

The example shown above is drawn in perspective, but other projections, such as **axonometric projection**, can also be used (see page 84).

Assignment: *Make a freehand exploded drawing of a small item, such as a child's constructional toy (e.g. Lego) or a torch.*

TEXTURE

Texture refers to the surface of a material and its **tactile** quality (what it 'feels like'). It can be most easily understood and described using the sense of **touch**. Surfaces can be smooth, fine, coarse, rough, etc. Different materials have different tactile qualities.

We only see that a surface is textured because of the effect of light and the shadows which it casts. If the light is at an angle to the surface, it will show the texture more clearly than if the same surface is directly lit.

Texture on an orange

How can you achieve the illusion of texture on a two-dimensional surface? One way is to take a **rubbing** using a pencil or wax crayon; but this method is not accurate enough for design drawings. Rubbings can, however, be effectively used for backgrounds to more accurate renderings.

Rubbed texture used to set-off a rendering of a stapler

The drawings on this page show examples of ways in which you can create the illusion of the surface texture of some common materials. It is most important that you try to observe carefully and, wherever possible, draw from the real thing, especially in the case of wood, which has many different grain effects. See page 50.

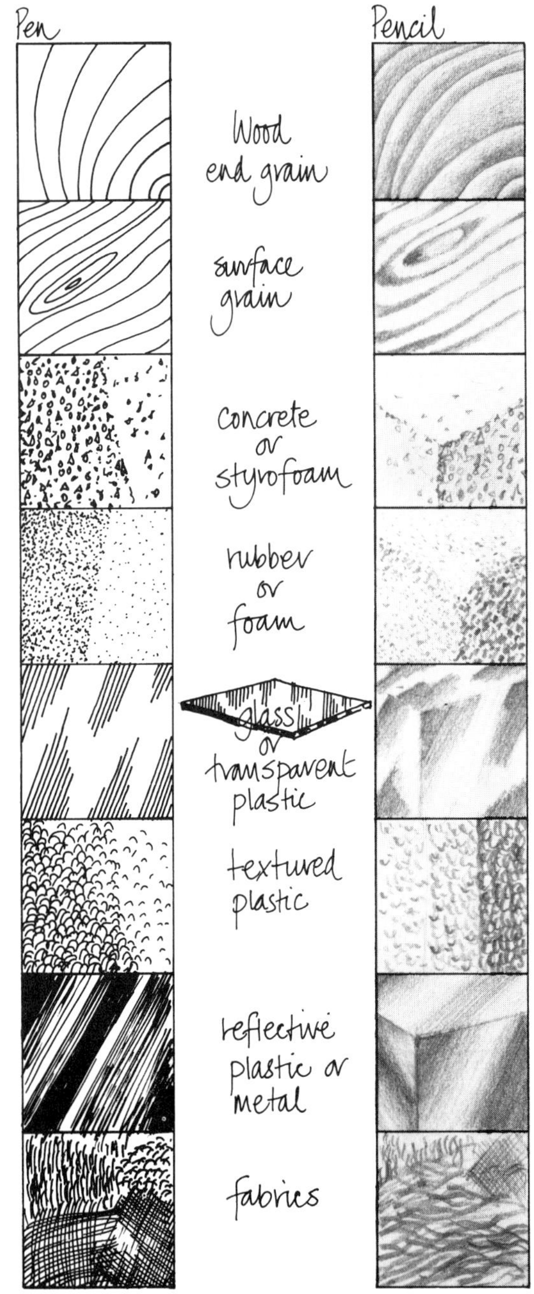

Assignment: *Draw several cubes and render each with a different texture. When you have done this, make a drawing of a small everyday object and render it to look as though it is made of a different material, e.g. make an aerosol can look as if it's made of wood, or a hammer as if it's made of rubber!*

Models and modelling

Models are a very important part of design because they allow us to communicate ideas in a three-dimensional form. They may be used to **demonstrate** how something works, to **mock-up** and develop an idea, or they may be a highly-finished **prototype** solution. Many different materials can be used to make models, ranging from card, paper cups, string and wire to more specialist materials such as styrofoam and high-density polystyrene.

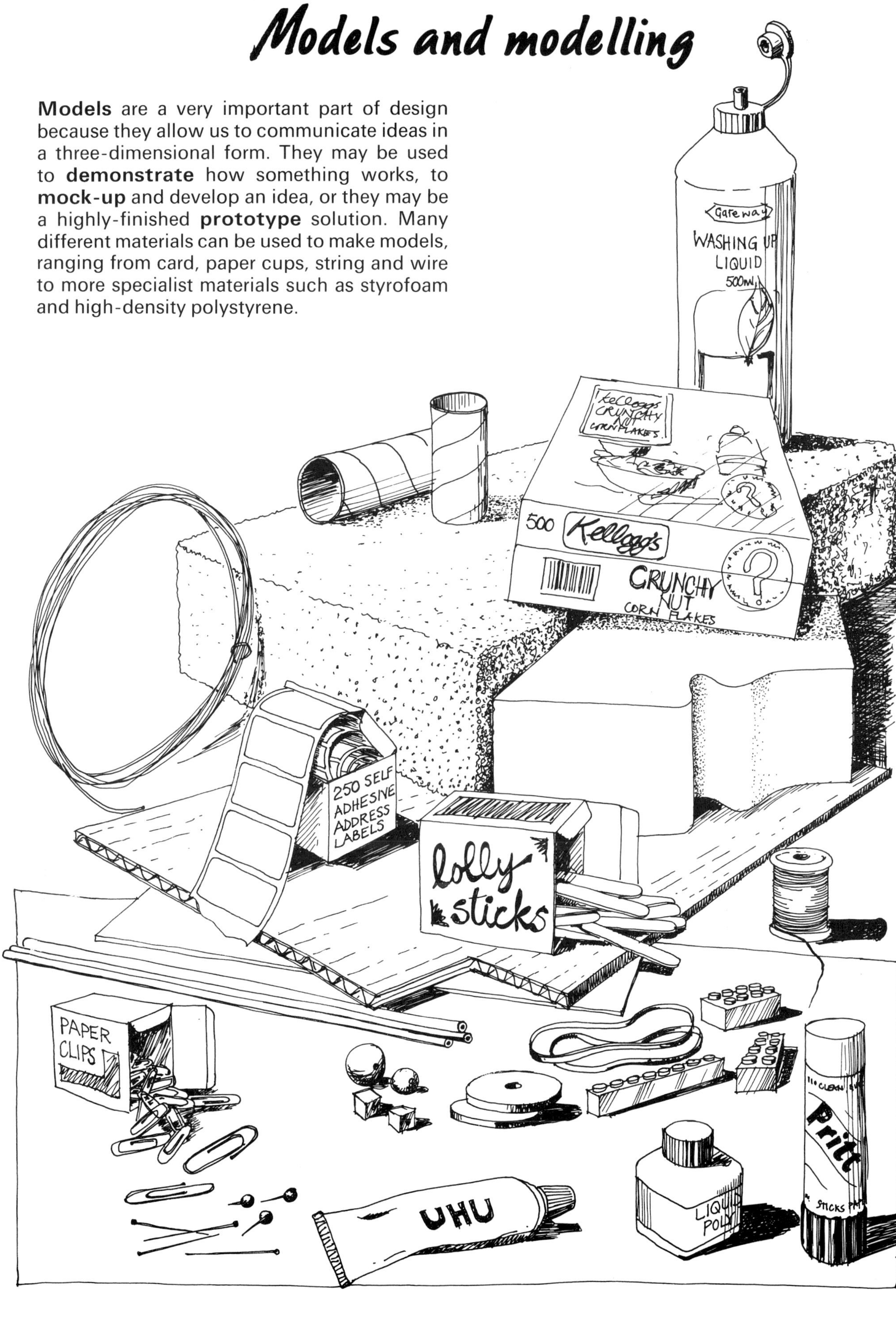

▸ DEVELOPING SHAPE INTO FORM

It is important that you understand the difference between shape and form. As you have seen, shape is two-dimensional: it has length and breadth, but no depth. It relates only to surface area. Form, on the other hand, can be thought of as a number of surface shapes in a **three-dimensional** arrangement, i.e., having length, breadth and depth.

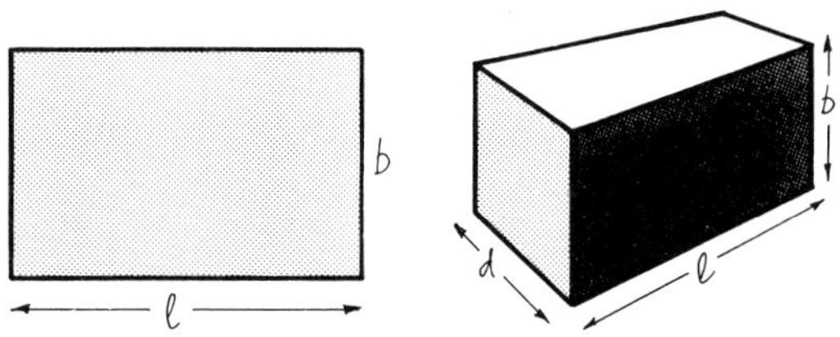

If you take a rectangular piece of stiff paper and fold it once, you will have created two smaller shapes. It is now possible for this paper to stand by itself on a surface, as it is three-dimensional. The more folds you put into the paper, the more **complex** the form will become.

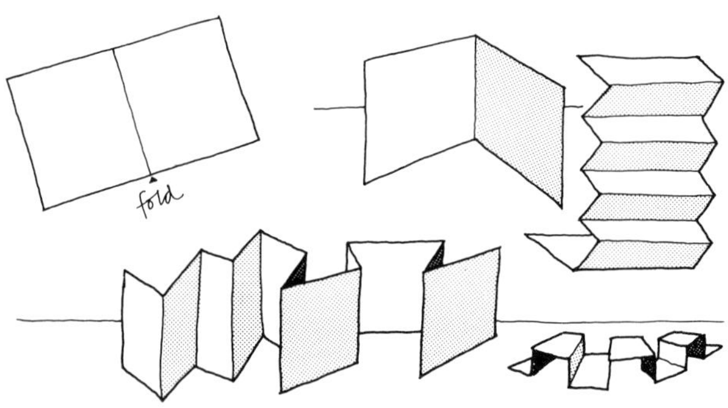

Folding creates form

The folding of flat paper and card has many everyday uses, the simplest of all being the greetings card. The **Pop-up image** is another example which is quite often used in the design of greetings cards and books to add an element of surprise.

▸ POP-UP IMAGES

There are many ways of making pop-up images. On the following pages, you will find visual instructions to enable you to make a **single layer pop-up**, a **multiple layer pop-up** and a **V-fold pop-up**. You will need stiff paper or card, scissors or a scalpel and a glue stick.

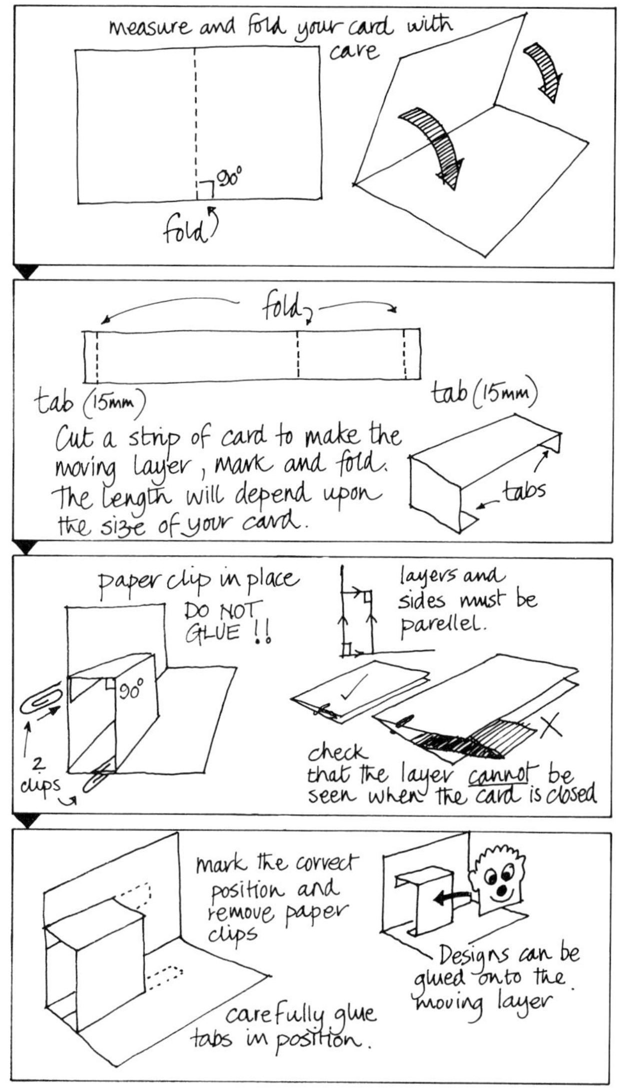

Single layer pop-up

Pop-up birthday card using a single layer and a 'V' fold

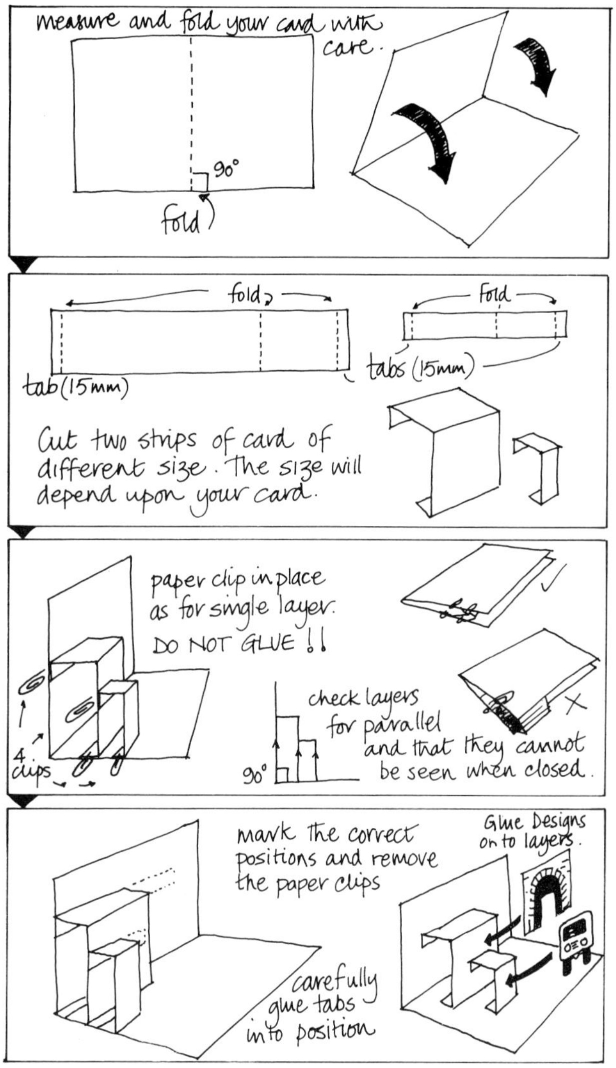

Multiple layer pop-up

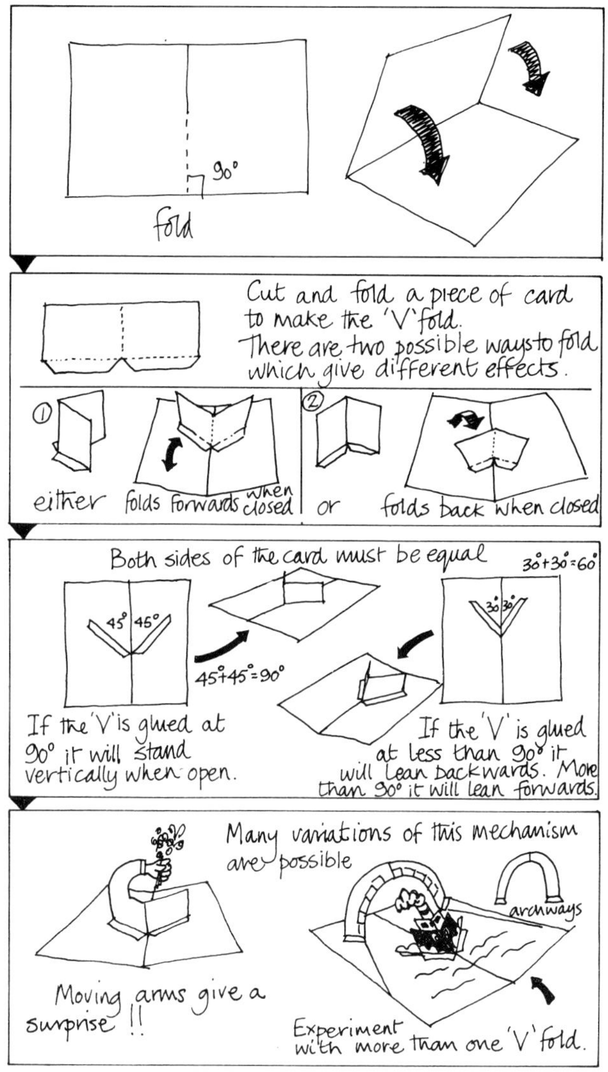

'V' fold pop-up

'V' fold pop-up in a book

When you are confident that you can make these three simple movements, you can then think about solving the next two assignments.

Assignment: *Using one or more pop-up mechanisms, design and make a humorous pop-up greetings card to surprise a friend.*

Assignment: *Young children like brightly-coloured picture books which use simple, bold shapes. Design a double page for an alphabet book which uses pop-up images. Use only one letter of the alphabet for each page.*

Many other forms can be created by folding paper and card. A **cube**, for example, can be thought of as six squares joined along their edges. When these shapes are opened out, they form a more complex shape. This is called a **development** of the form.

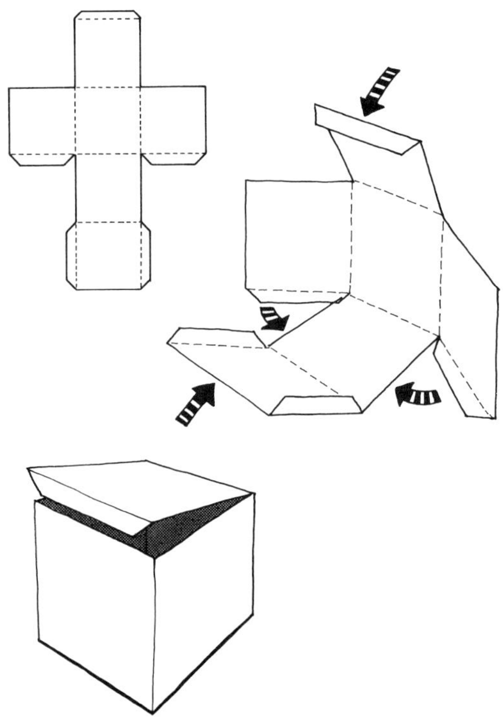

The diagram above shows one possible development for a cube. How many other ways can you develop it? Use a sheet of squared paper to help work out the possibilities. You will also have to work out the positions of the glueing tabs.

Assignment: *Work out the development for other forms, such as the cuboid, prism and pyramid. Test these developments by getting a friend to make them. Can they be improved upon?*

The process of creating **hollow forms** by folding up flat developments is used to produce many everyday articles. Perhaps the most obvious of these is the cardboard box, which is used for packaging everything from corn flakes to chocolates, and electric drills to computers. Look around you and see how many different types of box you can find. Open them out and sketch their developments. You will find that some are glued together whereas others rely on folding alone. They are not always cuboids, as you can see from the two photographs which follow.

Development of packaging used in a biscuit promotion

A development of this Easter egg box is shown on page 58

Developments must be drawn accurately if they are to work when cut out and folded up. You will need to use drawing instruments. If you turn to page 79, you will find more help with this.

Assignment: *Design a novelty box to hold an Easter egg. How can you support the Easter egg to stop it being broken?*

Assignment: *Many cereal manufacturers put cut-outs on the backs of their packages as an aid to marketing. Design a three-dimensional mask which can be folded up from a flat design printed on a cereal packet. The mask could be fierce, weird, comical, happy or sad. Produce both the cereal packet including the unfolded mask and a separate folded version of the mask. You may also need to include visual instructions on how the mask should be assembled.*

DEMONSTRATION MODELS

A **demonstration model** can be thought of as a 'moving drawing' which shows how a mechanism works and which can be made out of card or thin plywood. Simple demonstration models can show the four basic kinds of mechanical motion: **linear, reciprocating, oscillating** and **rotary**. These four mechanisms are quite often found in pop-up cards and books. Mechanisms can also be worked out from kits such as Lego Technic.

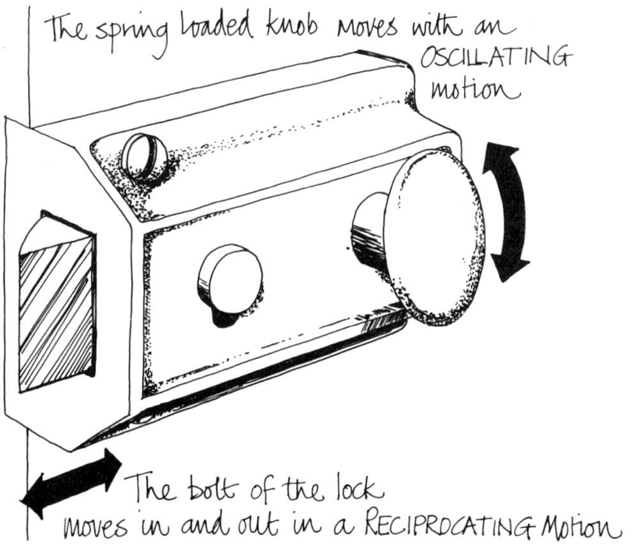

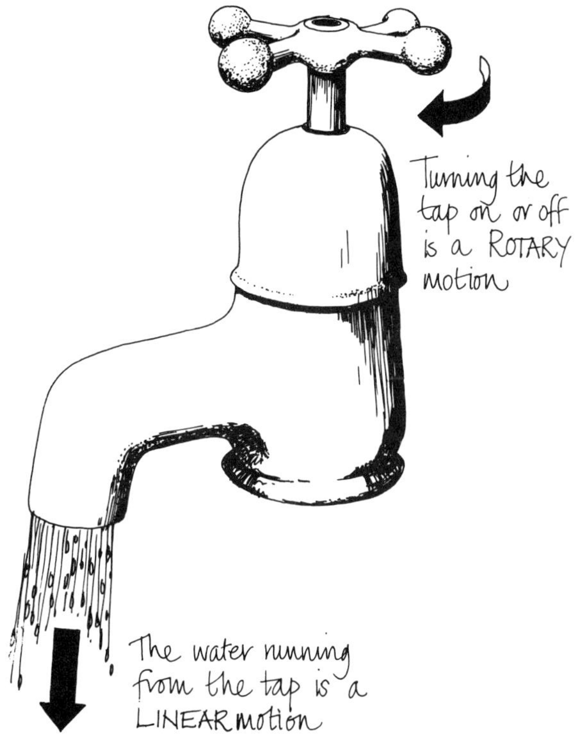

Models made from Lego Technic

Linear motion is movement in a straight line and can be achieved using a **slider** with a **pull-tab**. A slot is cut into a piece of card, bearing in mind the direction of movement required. Two smaller pieces of card are then folded in half and passed through the slot.

A strip of stiff card is then cut to act as the pull-tab, and this is glued carefully to the back of two smaller pieces.

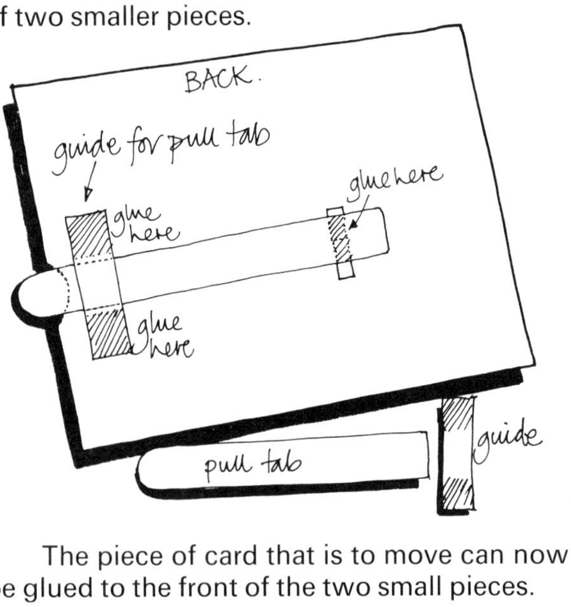

The piece of card that is to move can now be glued to the front of the two small pieces.

By pulling the tab, the linear motion is achieved. An element of surprise can be added by making the moving image come from behind a screen.

Reciprocating motion is the same as linear motion, except that the movement here is backwards and forwards. This can be achieved in exactly the same way as linear motion, using a pull-tab.

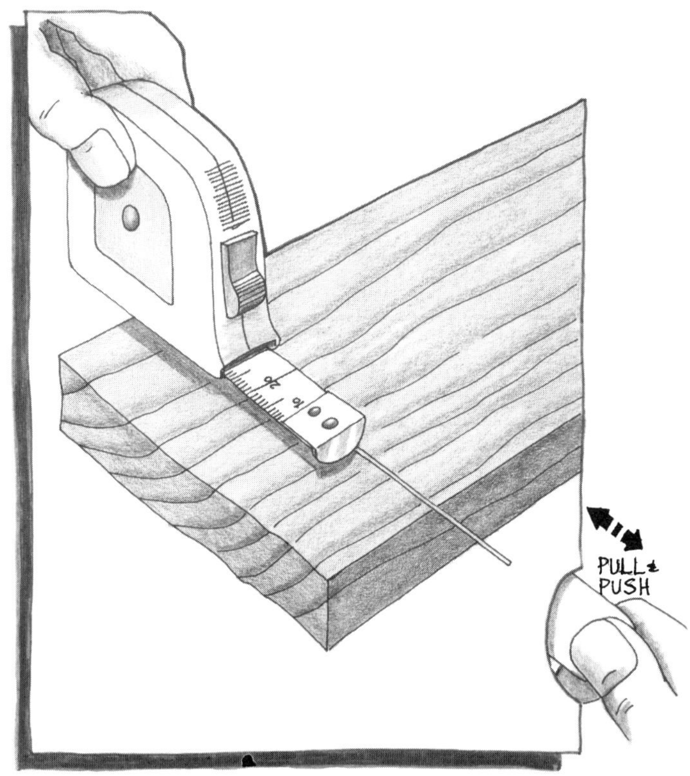

Reciprocating motion is used to move the tape measure

Assignment: *Design and make a simple pull-tab model to demonstrate an everyday activity which involves linear or reciprocating motion. The visual appearance must be attractive and carefully thought-out if the model is to be effective.*

Rotary motion is circular, like a turning wheel. In the example on this page, the clown's bow tie rotates.

From another piece of card, cut out a disc 30 mm in diameter. Mark this out and then cut and fold it as shown below.

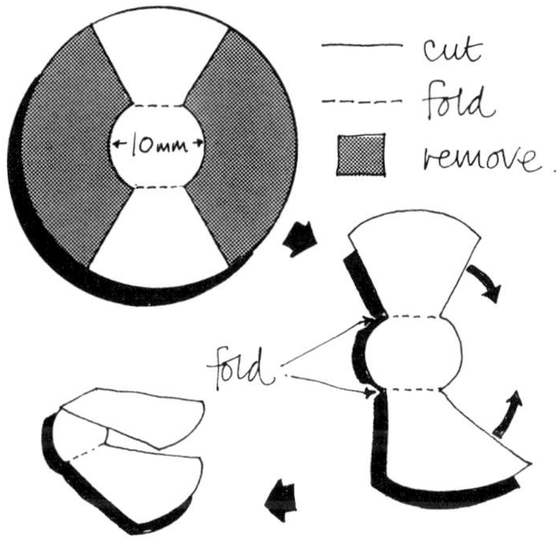

Stick the centre of the tabs to the back of the part that is to move (in this case, the bow tie). If you glue off-centre, you will create a cam effect. What is a cam? What does a cam do?

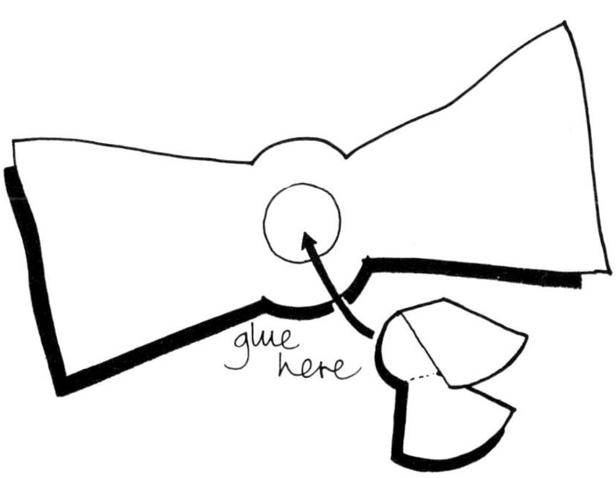

Now cut a larger circle of card which is just big enough to overlap the edge of the main design. Pass the tabs through the hole and glue them to the centre of the disc.

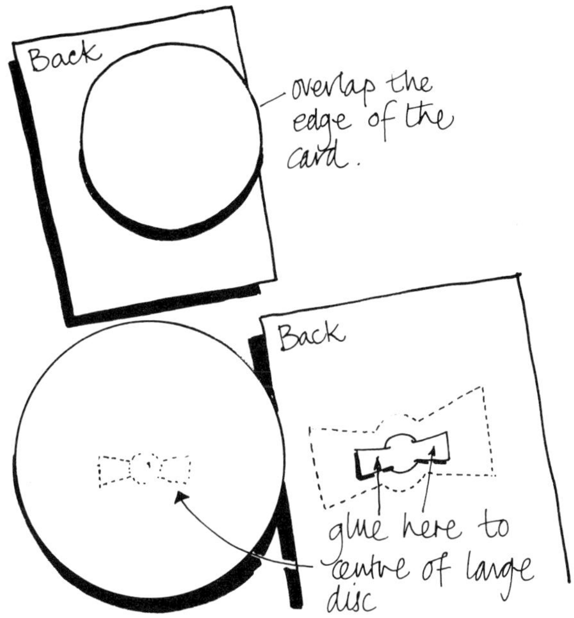

By turning the edge of the large disc with your finger, the rotary motion can be achieved.

Obviously, this mechanism must be carefully designed and accurately made if it is to work well. More complicated rotary models can be made from plywood and dowel rod to show how things like cogs and gearwheels work.

Assignment: *Design and make an amusing model to demonstrate rotary motion.*

Oscillating motion is also circular, but it is a backwards and forwards motion, in an arc movement. It can be achieved in the same way as rotary motion or by using a **pivot** and **tab**.

To produce a pivot and tab model, you must first decide on the size of arc you wish to use and draw part of it on the card using compasses. Then punch a small hole through the centre point (where the compass point has been) and cut a curved slot along the arc.

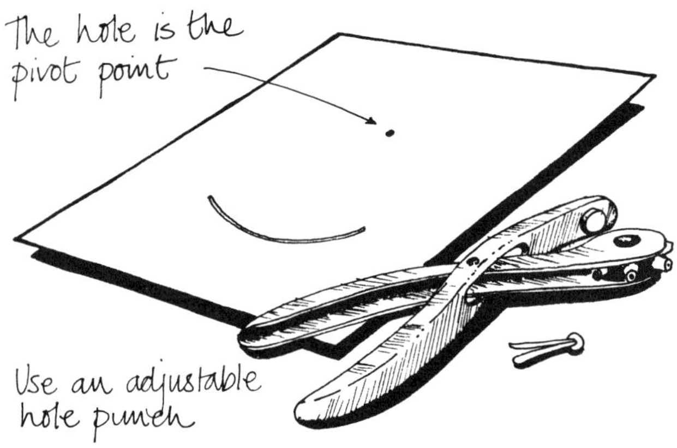

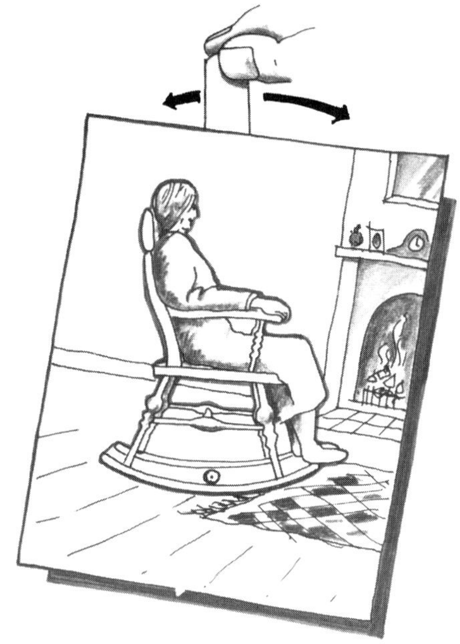

The motion is achieved by moving the tab back and forth. As with rotary motion, you must design and make your mechanism very carefully if it is to be successful. Different motions can be combined together to demonstrate more complex actions and activities.

Next, cut a strip of stiff card which is long enough to reach from the centre of the circle to the edge of the card. Punch a hole in one end of this strip. The image to be moved is then cut and punched and the three pieces are held together with a bifurcated rivet.

A small piece of card is then cut and folded in half, passed through the slot and carefully glued to the tab and image.

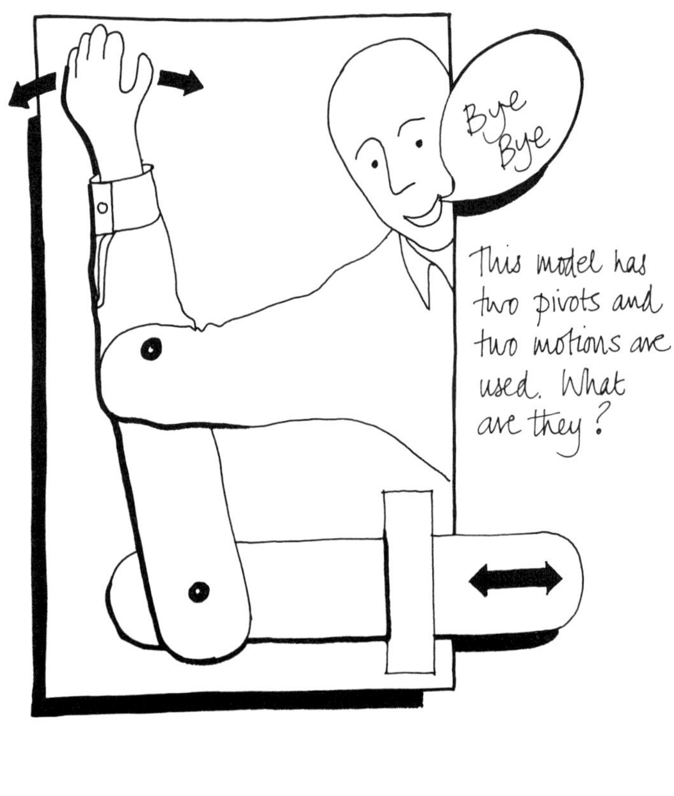

***Assignment**: Design and make a model which demonstrates both oscillating and linear motion. Look at the actions involved in ball games for ideas. The model is to be used to explain these motions to young children in primary school.*

MOCK-UPS

It is almost impossible to visualize form completely in two-dimensions. **Mock-ups** are therefore used to help the designer experiment with **size** and **proportion**, and with **ergonomics** (the positions of details such as switches and handles).

Depending on what is being designed, the mock-up may be full size or scaled down (smaller than full size). For example, a mock-up camera would most likely be full size, whilst a mock-up chair would usually be scaled down.

A wide variety of materials is available for making mock-ups. **Card** and **stiff paper** can be used for packaging; **wire** for frameworks; **clay** and **Plasticine** for moulding; **balsa** and **woods** can be used for more detailed work, but can be difficult to handle. A material which can be used to get accurate mock-ups fairly quickly is **styrofoam.**

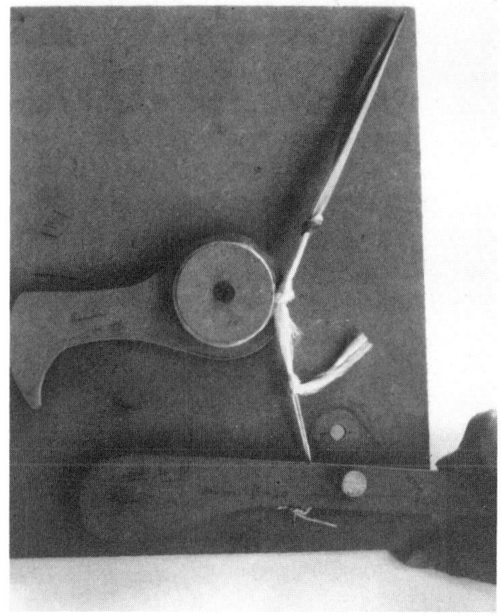

A mock-up made from fibre-board in order to test a mechanism

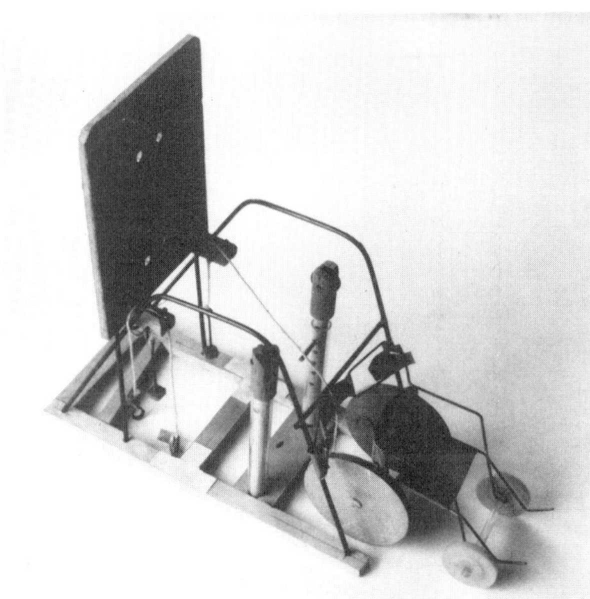

Mock-up of a weight-training station for disabled children made with wire, card and plywood

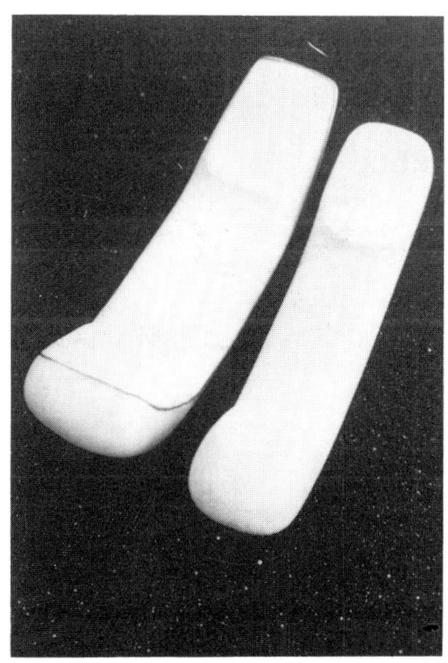

Styrofoam telephone mock-ups

▸ USING STYROFOAM

Styrofoam is a rigid plastic foam which is easily cut and shaped using ordinary hand tools. When using styrofoam the side view of the design is transferred to the styrofoam using a **paper template**, and the shape can then be cut using either a small handsaw or a bandsaw.

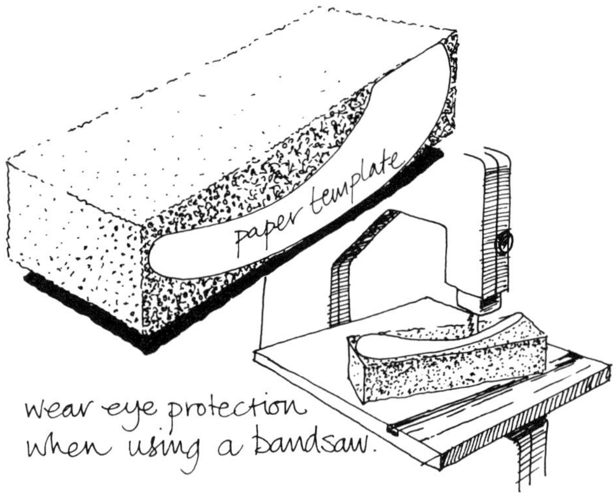

The form can then be developed further by filing and finally sanding. This process creates fine particles and it is advisable to wear a face mask.

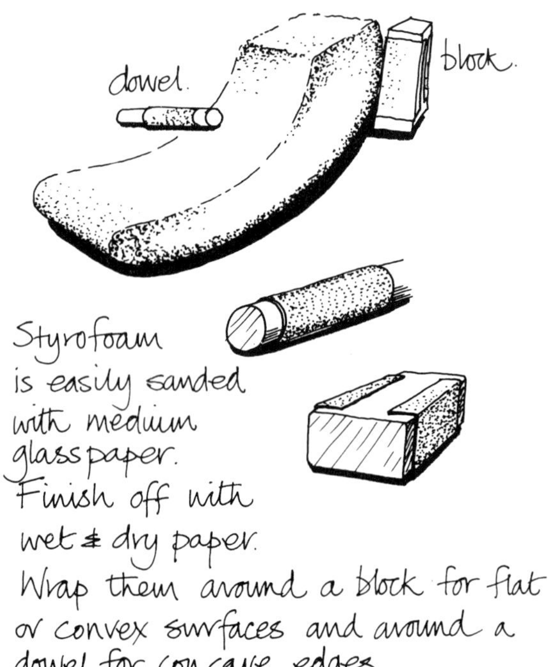

Smaller details can be cut out and glued-on with PVA or double sided tape. The model can be painted with emulsion paint if colour is required.

NB: Do not use impact adhesive such as EvoStik or cellulose-based paints as they will eat into the surface of the styrofoam.

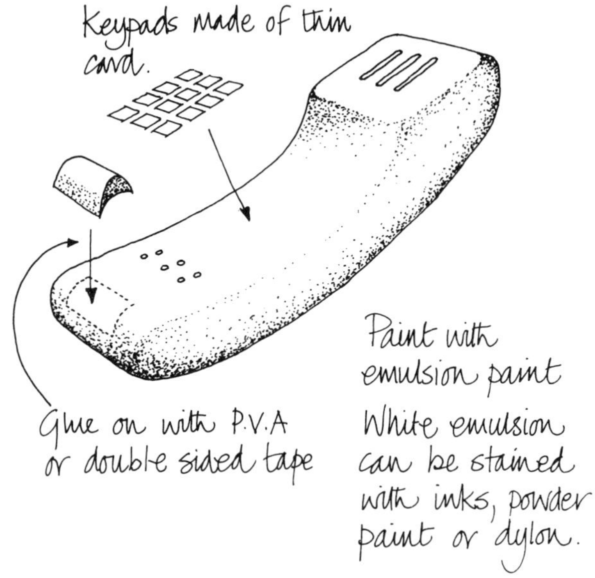

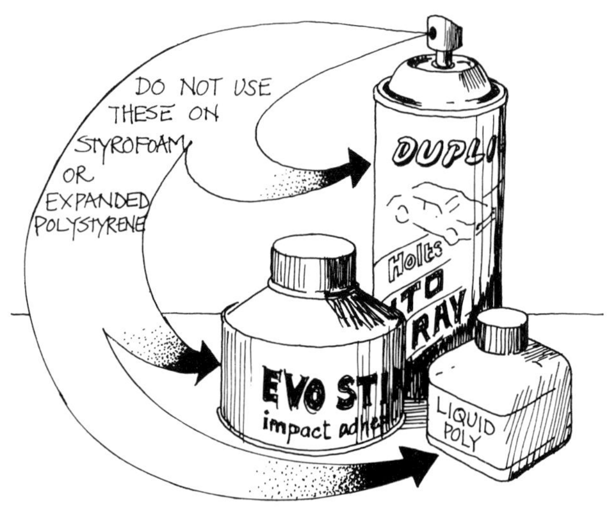

Assignment: *Make a careful study of examples of the many new designs for telephones that are now available. From your research, develop a design for a one-piece telephone. Mock-up your ideas in styrofoam to help you finalize the design.*

FINAL VISUAL MODELS

The final visual model can be made from a material called **high density expanded polystyrene**. This material is worked in exactly the same way as styrofoam, but gives a very smooth surface when sanded.

High density expanded polystyrene can be bonded with PVA glue, but impact adhesives should not be used. It can, however, be sprayed with cellulose paint to obtain a fine finish as long as the surface has been **sealed** first. Sealing can be accomplished using **emulsion paint** which has been mixed with a little **plaster of Paris**.

Remember to wear a face mask when sanding and to spray in a well ventilated space.

Split lines can be introduced on to the surface of a visual model to simulate the edges where two mouldings meet.

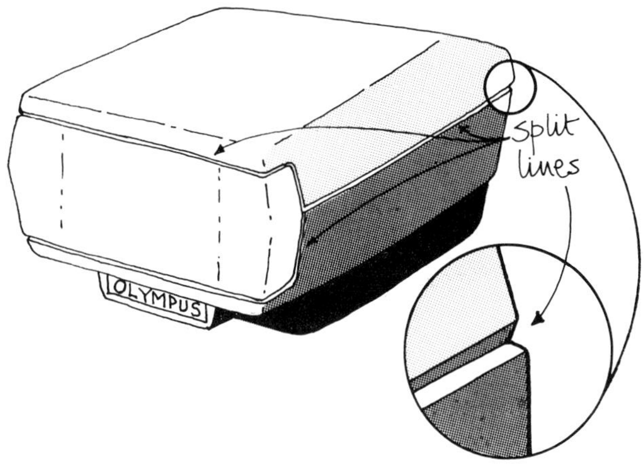

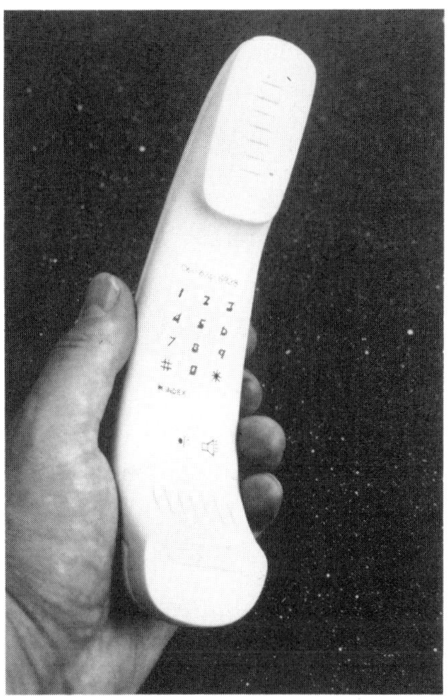

High density expanded polystyrene phone model, with surface detailing added using self-adhesive labels

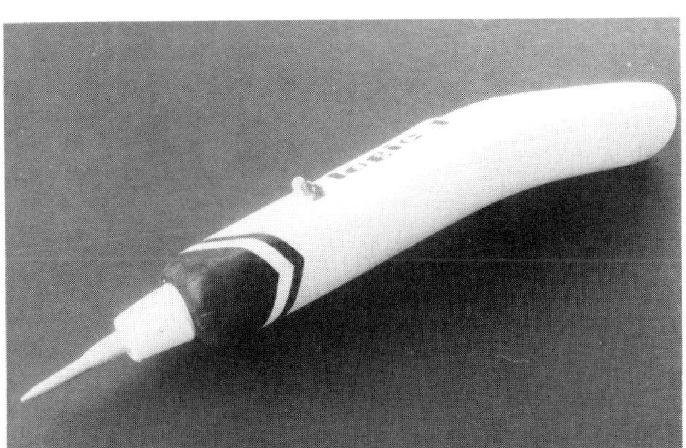

Logic tester in high density expanded polystyrene

Scale model of a knock-down seat, using plywood

Final visual models can also be made from wood, such as jellutong, or plastic sheet, such as **high impact polystyrene**.

Assignment: *Make a detailed final visual model of your design for a one-piece telephone.*

▸ SIMULATING SURFACE DETAIL

As finished visual models must appear to be 'the real thing', surface detail is most important. For example, plastic articles quite often have textured finishes and lettering moulded into them. These can be simulated very effectively using a variety of simple and easily-obtained materials which, when stuck on to the surface of the model and sprayed over, appear to be moulded in.

Self-adhesive paper labels can be used to create a number of effects, such as speaker grills and battery covers. Other textured surfaces can be obtained by glueing on fine **wet and dry paper** or Slater's **Plastikard**.

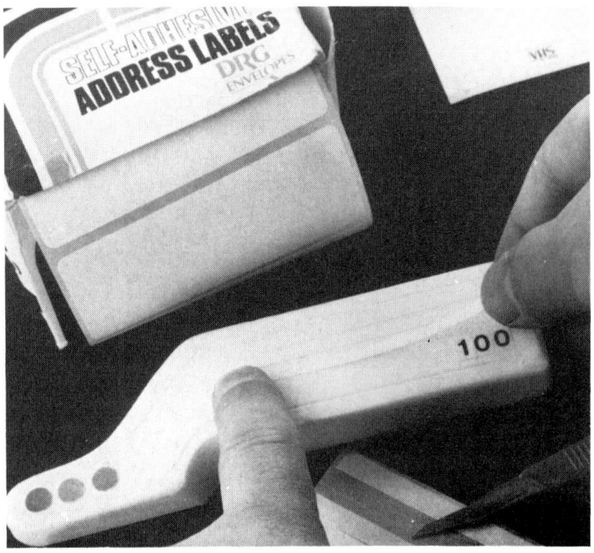

Positioning surface detail cut from self-adhesive labels

Detail of a battery cover simulated by cutting a self-adhesive address label into the shape of an arrow

Lettering can be added in three ways. You can use: modeller's **plastic letters, die-cut self-adhesive letters**, or **dry transfer lettering**.

Die-cut self-adhesive letters can be applied before or after spraying, depending on the desired effect. Dry transfer lettering should be used after spraying.

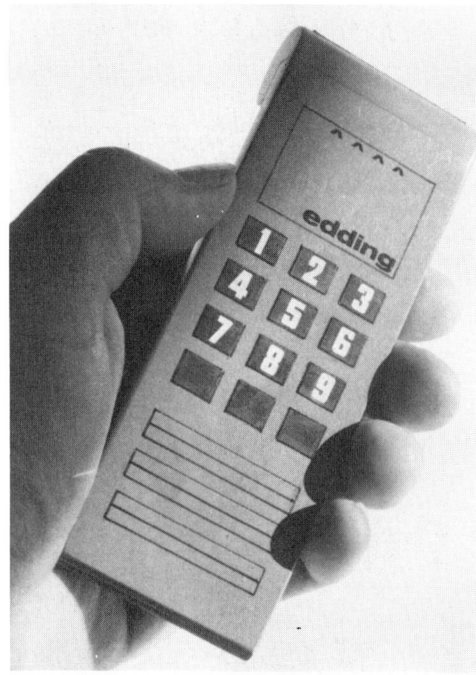

This plywood model of an infra-red handset uses both instant and die-cut lettering and labels

Modeller's plastic letters can be applied to polystyrene sheet using liquid polystyrene solvent. If the letters are to contrast with the surface, this can be achieved by rubbing lightly with wet and dry paper after spraying.

NB: Modeller's plastic letters cannot be applied to high density polystyrene (see under Visual Models).

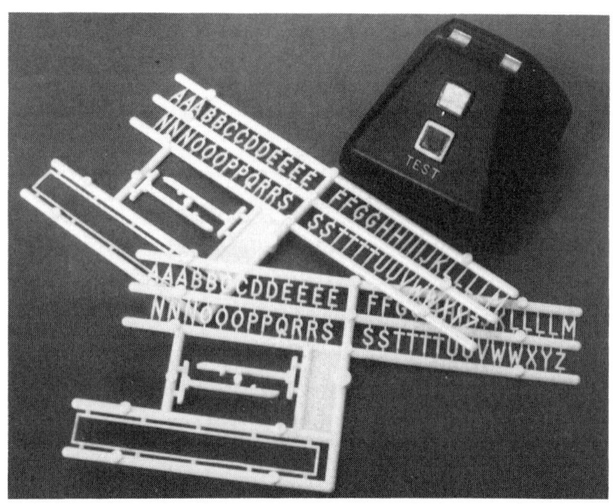

Modeller's plastic letters for use on high impact polystyrene

PROTOTYPES

A prototype is a model of the final design which is not only accurate visually, but which also works.

High impact polystyrene sheet is excellent for producing working prototypes for articles which would be mass produced by **injection moulding**. It can be easily worked and **fabricated** using hand tools or it can be **vacuum formed** into more complex forms. It will accept a variety of texturing and colouring sprays.

▸ FABRICATION

Shapes can be marked out on the surface of the plastic using a sharp pencil or fine liner. They can then be cut out either by **scoring** and **snapping** if the edges are straight, or by **sawing** around curves. The parts can be filed and sanded to obtain an accurate fit.

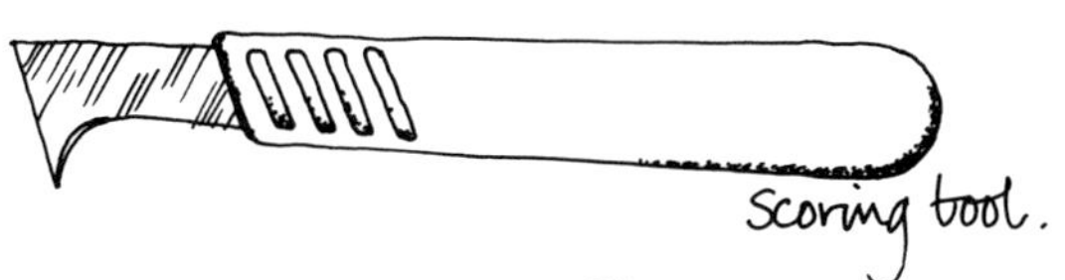

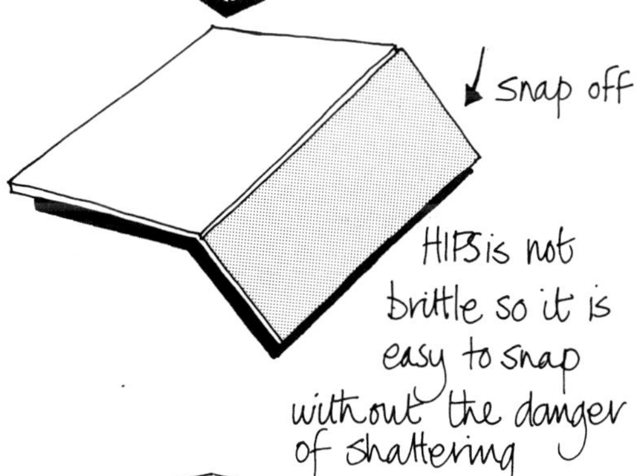

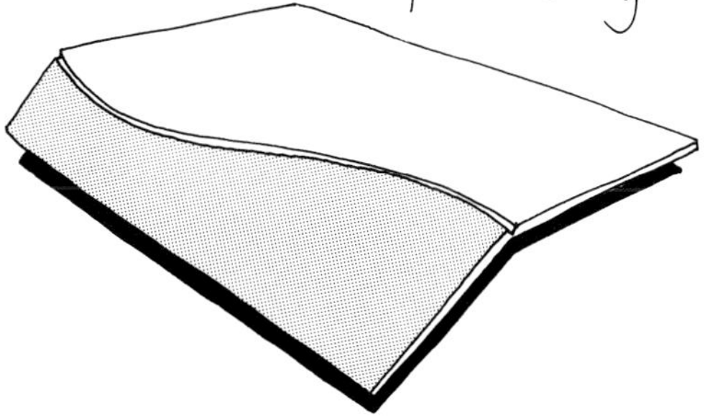

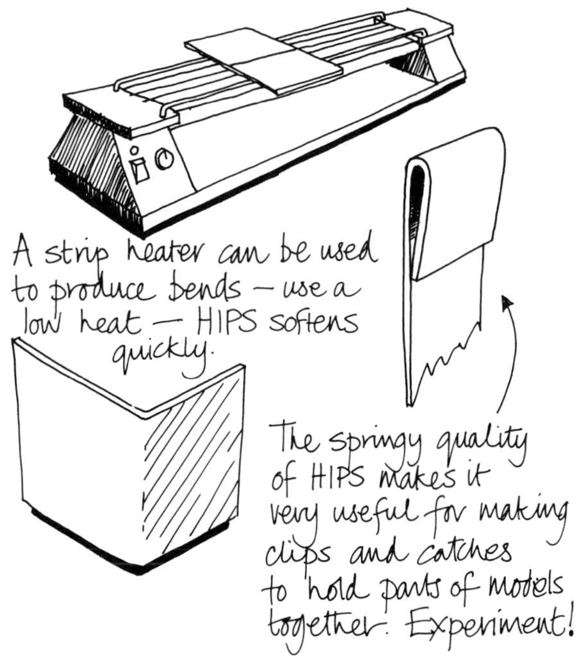

The edges to be joined should be placed together and a small amount of solvent brushed along the join. **Capillary action** pulls the solvent between the two parts and **fuses** them together.

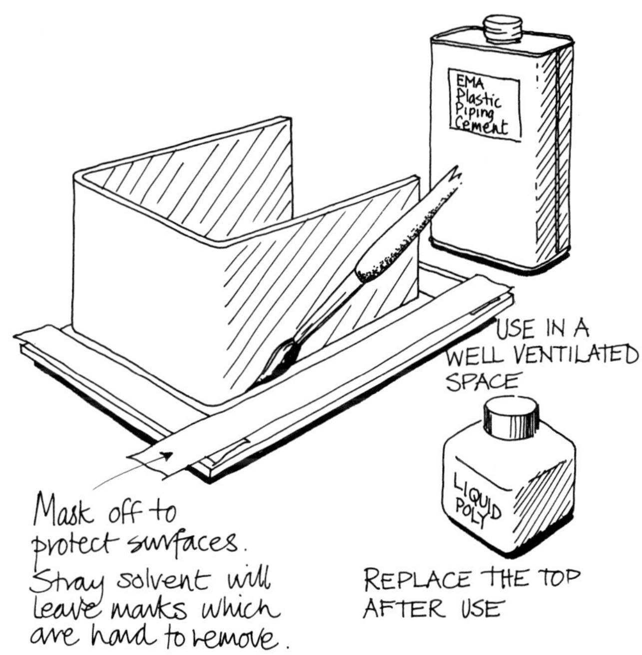

Assignment*: Design and fabricate from high impact polystyrene a novelty pencil sharpener, which has a container for shavings. You must consider carefully how you will position the sharpener and how you will remove the shavings. Make careful drawings so that you can mark out the materials accurately. What kind of drawing would be best for this?*

▸ VACUUM FORMING

High impact polystyrene is a **thermoplastic**. Thermoplastics are useful because they can be softened by heating and then moulded. It is not necessary to have expensive equipment to soften them: a simple vacuum-former can be made from plywood and an old vacuum cleaner and a hot air paint stripper will provide a heat source. Your teacher will be able to tell you more about this technique.

Small electrical prototypes can be made by vacuum-forming a casing in two parts and then fitting a circuit. The circuit has to be considered carefully first. It is necessary to work out the amount of space it will need before the casing can be designed.

When the design is finalized, an accurate wooden model or mould is made from an easily-worked hardwood such as **jellutong**. This model is then cut along the split line and a piece of 6 mm plywood is added to each part. This makes the mould slightly deeper to allow for trimming the plastic.

Wooden model for vacuum forming

The moulds can now be placed in the vacuum-former and the plastic heated and formed around them.

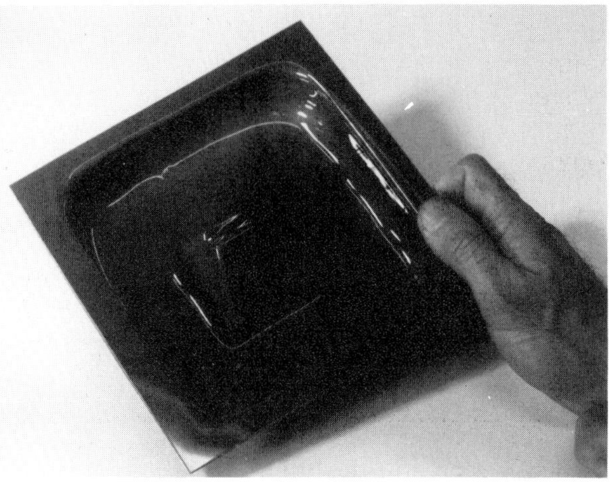

The two plastic parts can then be trimmed and fitted together. Locating clips can be fabricated and bonded to each part.

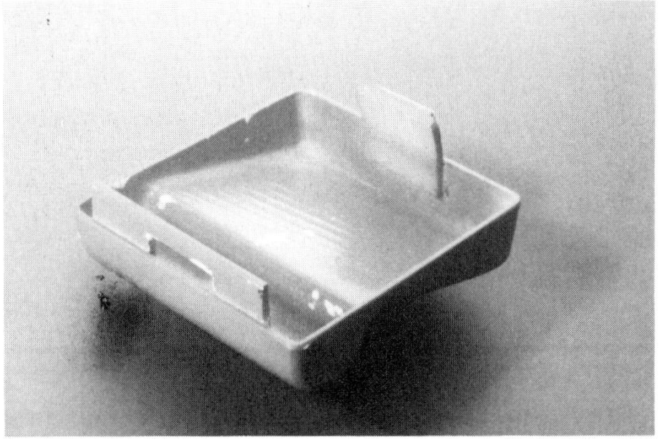

Finally, the circuit can be introduced.

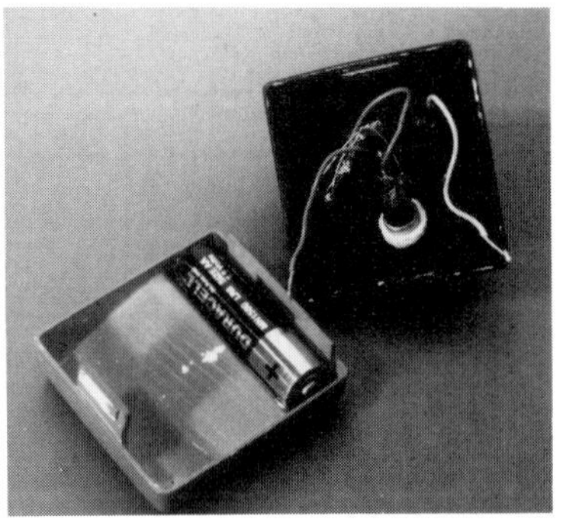

***Assignment**: Design and make an electronic timing device suitable for use in the kitchen. The casing is to be vacuum-formed from high impact polystyrene.*

▸ BLISTER PACKING

Nowadays, small articles are often sold in **blister packs** instead of card boxes. This type of packaging usually consists of a backing card with the article enclosed in a clear plastic blister. It allows the article to be displayed, so that customers can see exactly what they are buying.

Blister packaging

The blister, which is vacuum-formed, is sometimes a simple box, but it can also follow the form of the article it encloses.

Blister pack and (right) display stand. The stand is made from plastic-coated wire

The design of the backing card is very important, as is the position of the article and blister. Quite often, a standard company style is used for all items, as well as a special display. This is known as a '**point-of-sale**' display.

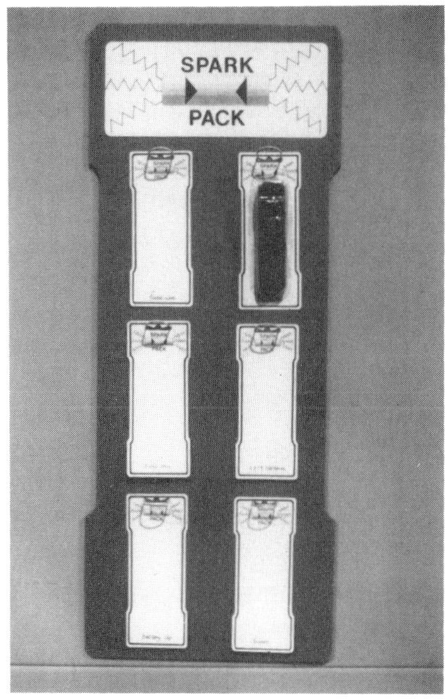

The design of this display panel was based on the shape of a cartridge fuse

Look around your local shops for examples of blister packaging. How many different kinds of article can you find? How are they displayed?

Assignment*: Design some blister packaging and a point-of-sale display for a firm which produces such things as pencil sharpeners, mini staplers, drawing pins, hole punches, etc. Make one full-size blister pack for your novelty pencil sharpener and a scale model of the display stand.*

Production drawings

Production or **working drawings** are accurate drawings which are followed exactly when making the final design. This kind of drawing is used widely by the manufacturing industry, architects, builders and individual craftspeople. The Victorians used to tint the different parts of their drawings, but when the **dyeline** process of printing drawings was invented, the copies that were made appeared blue, giving rise to the term **blueprint**.

Originally, the designer passed on his ideas to the **draughtsman**, who then drew the final production drawing to scale. Nowadays, computers are gradually taking over the draughtsman's role and can be directly used by the designer to produce a vast range of information about the product.

For example, they allow the designer to draw and rotate the object through 360° on the screen, to alter parts, to zoom in and out and to print out many different views of the final design. This is known as **computer-aided design (CAD)**. Computers are now being developed that can even produce plastic models of the object being designed.

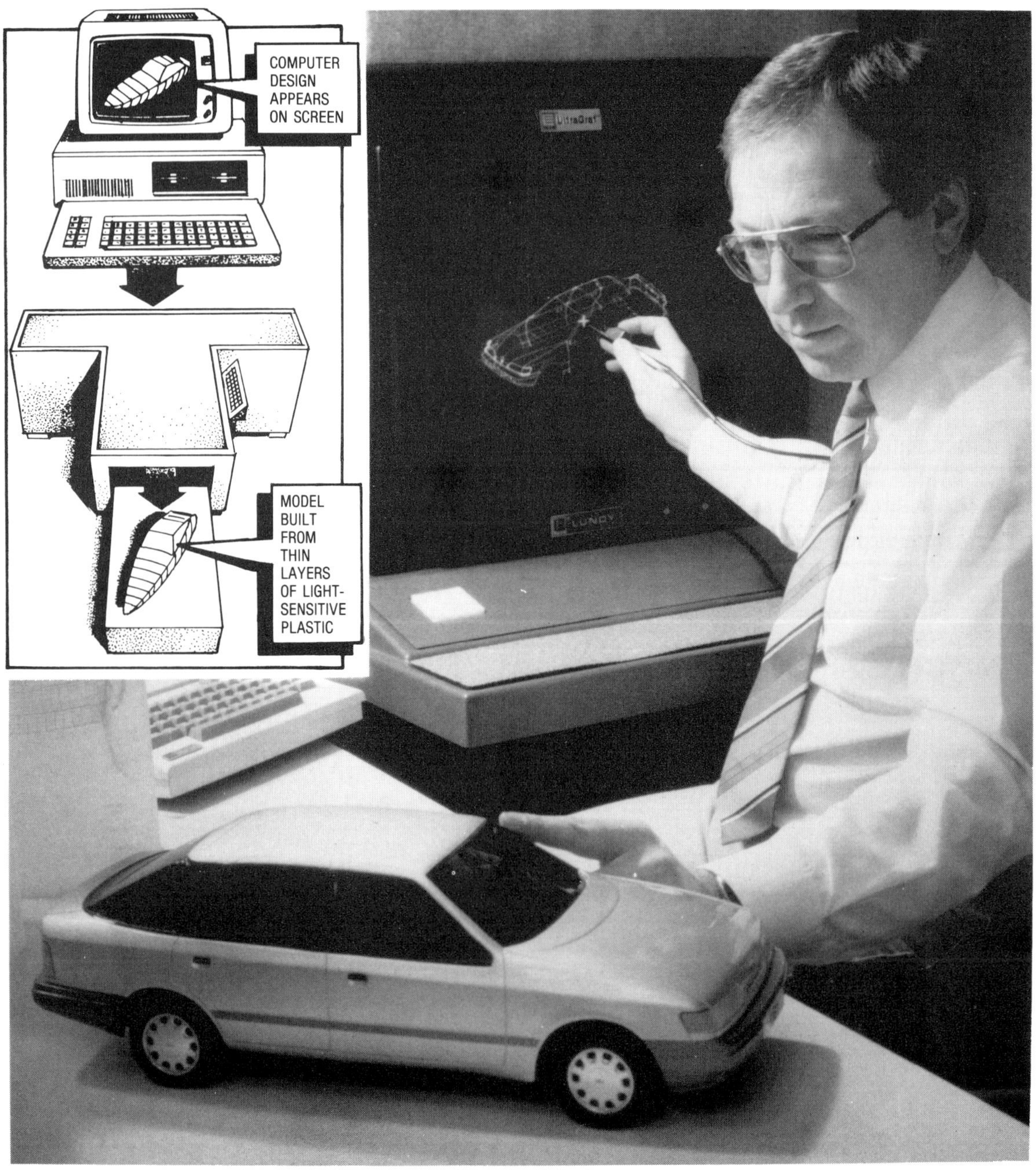

EQUIPMENT

To make a production drawing, you will need a drawing board with **T-square** or **parallel motion**; you will also need **set squares** and instruments, such as a **compass** and **rule**.

Before you start work, always make sure that your drawing equipment and your hands are clean. Fix your paper to the drawing board with tape or clips. Never use drawing pins as they damage the surface of the board. Some new plastic drawing units have a magnetic clip to hold paper.

If you are using a T-square, make sure it runs smoothly against the left-hand edge of the board. Use the top edge of it for drawing all horizontal lines.

When you use set squares, make certain that they rest against the top edge of your T-square.

It is important to use **hard pencils** for accurate measured drawings as they will retain a sharp point and give an even width of line. A **2H** pencil is adequate for most work of this kind.

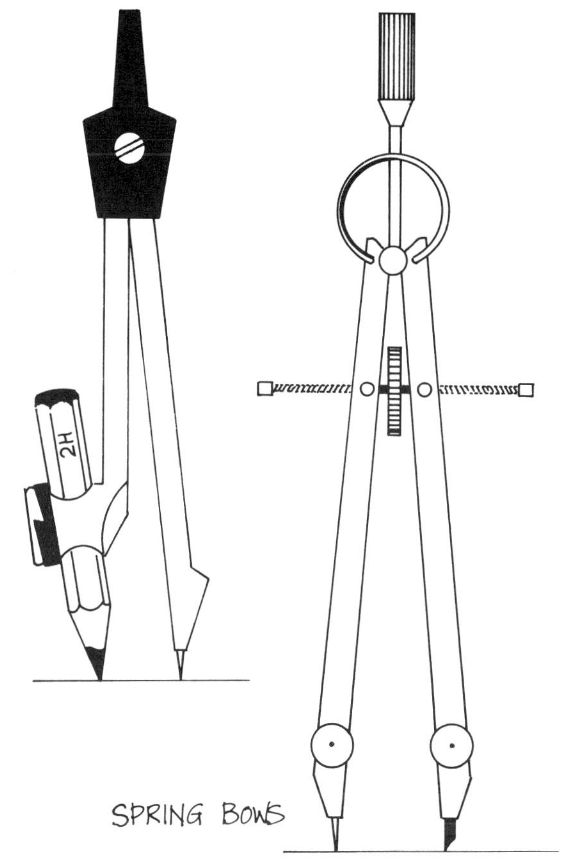

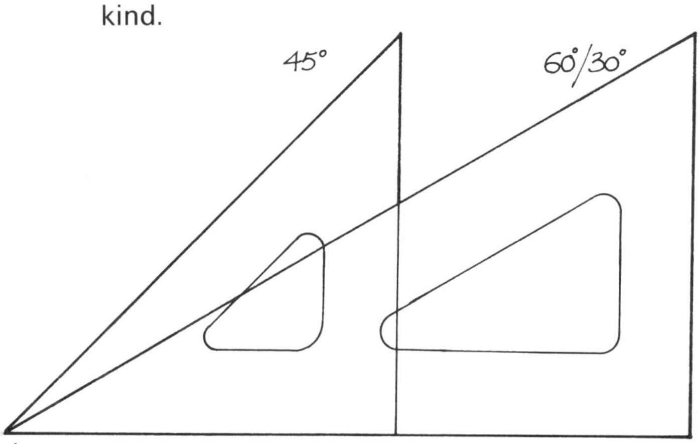

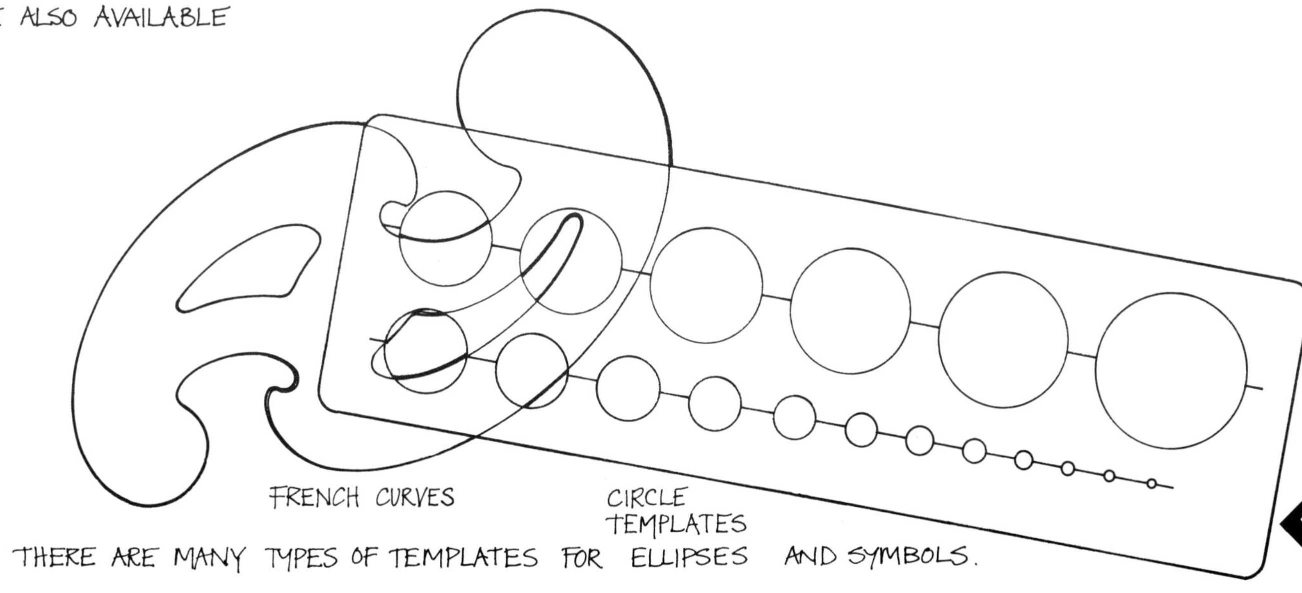

MEASURED ORTHOGRAPHIC PROJECTION

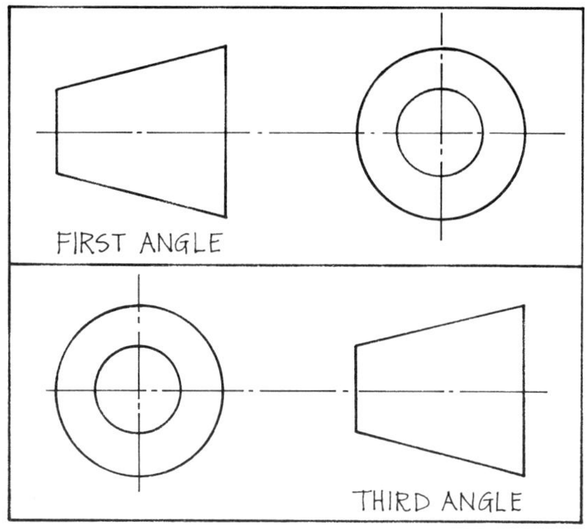

You have learned the principles of orthographic drawing without using instruments (page 23). *Measured* orthographic projection is a method of showing the true shapes and sizes of an object using elevations.

It is not difficult to make a measured orthographic drawing. First, you must decide which angle of projection you wish to use: first angle or third angle. Each of these projections is defined by its own symbol, which should be used on the drawing.

You must then decide on the scale of your drawing. This will depend on the size of your paper and also the size of the object to be drawn. For example, if you are using A3 paper, a music cassette tape could be scaled up in size, a VHS video cassette could be drawn full size, whilst a video recorder would need to be scaled down.

Remember that if you are scaling up or down, all the measurements must be altered by the same factor. If the drawing is to be twice full size, *all* measurements must be multiplied by two. If the drawing is to be a quarter scale, *all* measurements must be divided by four.

Different-sized objects need to be drawn to different scales

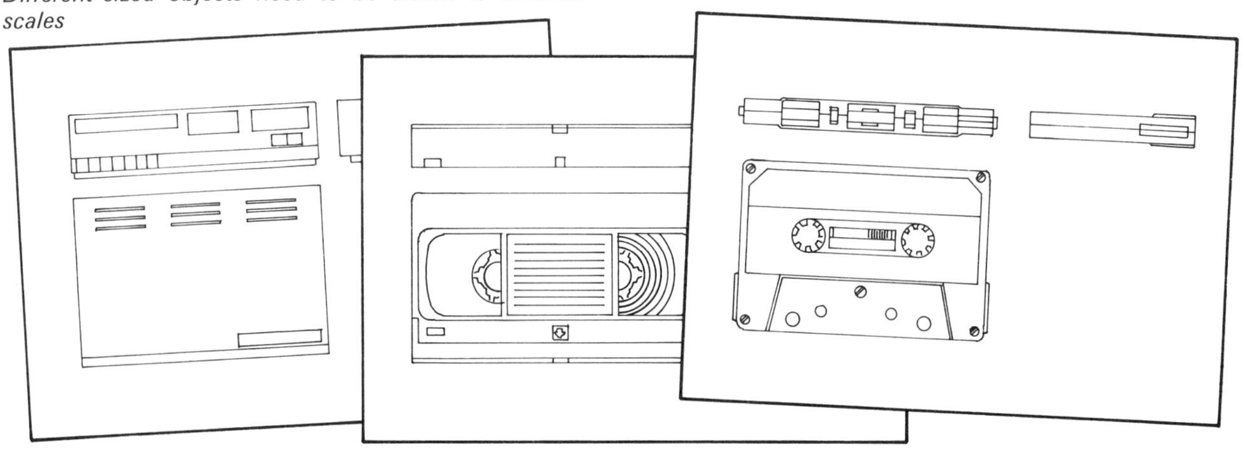

There are five types of line used in production drawings:

1 **Construction lines** are feint lines which are used to plan out the drawing.
2 **Outlines** are heavier lines which are drawn-in to denote all visible edges of surfaces, holes, etc.
3 **Hidden detail lines** are short dashes of equal length and spacing which show a hidden edge or a hole passing through an object.
4 **Centre lines** are alternate lines and dots which denote the centre line of a symmetrical object such as a cylinder.
5 **Dimension lines** are fine lines which show the measurement between two points.

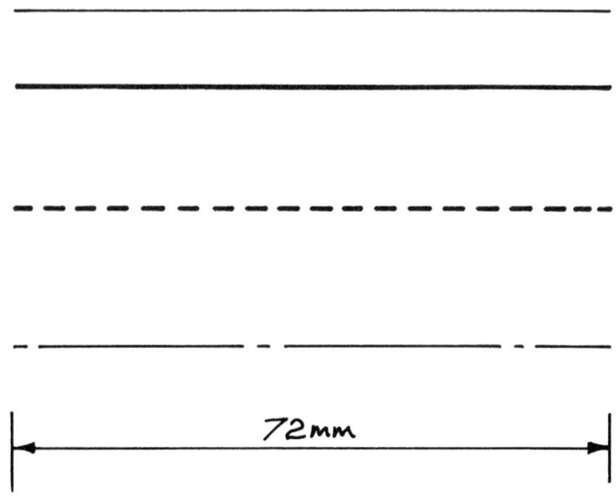

▸ FIRST ANGLE PROJECTION

First, make a freehand orthographic drawing of the object. Decide on the size and scale of your drawing in relation to the size of paper you are using. Then follow the procedure below, using construction lines only. Use a T-square for all horizontal lines and a T-square and set square combined for all vertical and 45° lines.

1 Draw the *x* and *y* axes on the paper, allowing enough room for the elevations to go in the correct positions without appearing squashed. Draw another line at 45° from the point where the *x* and *y* axes cross.

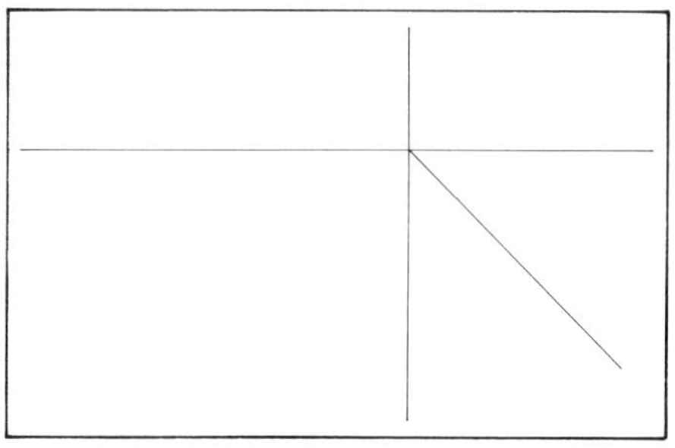

2 Draw a line parallel and a short distance above the *x* axis (10 mm above is adequate). This is the base line of the side and end elevations. Now do the same below the *x* axis.

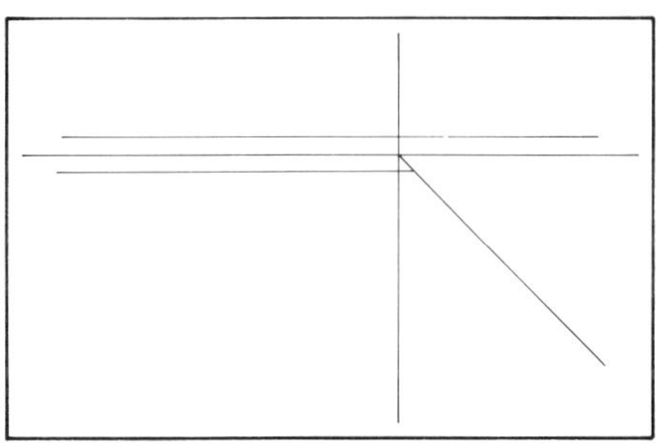

3 Draw a horizontal line above the base line. The distance between this line and the base line is the height of the object.

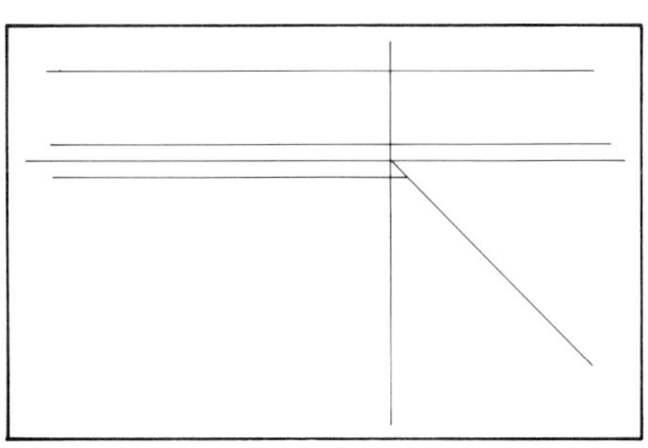

4 Draw another horizontal line underneath the one drawn below the *x* axis. The distance between these two lines is the width of the object.

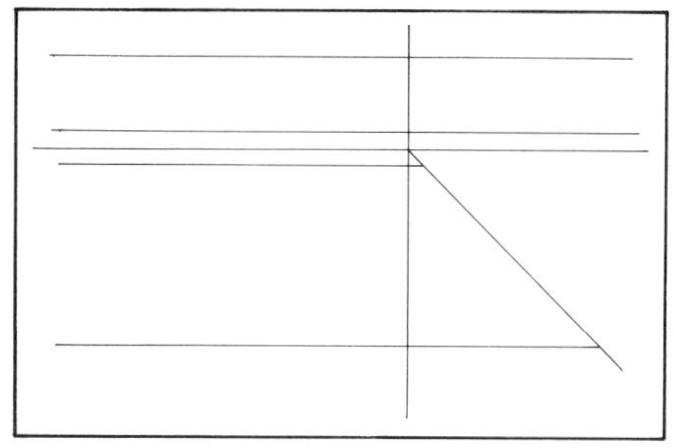

5 Draw a vertical line to the left of the *y* axis, using the same measurement as you used for the line drawn in **2** above. Draw another vertical line to the left of the one you have just drawn. The distance between these two lines is the length of the side of the object. Next, draw vertical lines from the points where the horizontals meet the diagonal line. You should now have drawn the basic side, end and plan elevations.

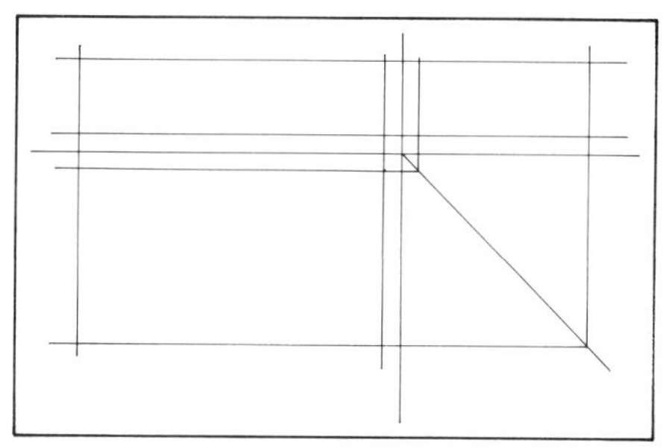

6 You can now draw-in each elevation with a heavier outline.

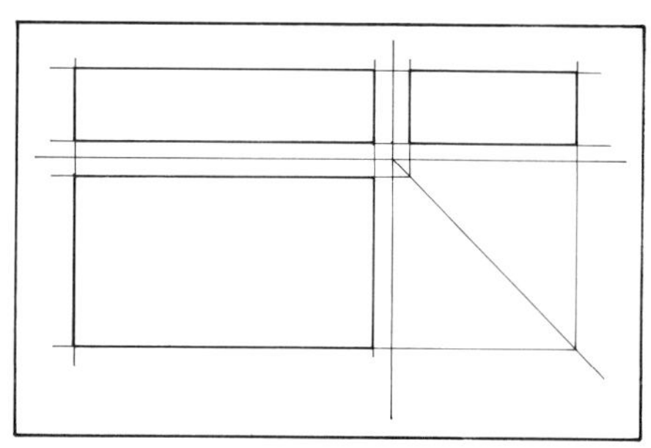

▸ 'DIMENSIONING'

There are a number of standard rules which you should follow when adding dimensions to your drawings. These rules have been devised by the British Standards Institute (BSI) and some examples of the standard style for giving dimensions can be seen on the drawing of the cam-operated toy below. The complete set of rules are given in the BSI's booklet number PD7 308.

The advantage of having a standard set of rules (rather than everyone simply using their own style) is that drawings made by different people can always be easily and quickly understood.

All dimensions should be clearly written and each one should appear only once on the drawing. Note how the circles have been dimensioned, and the shape and size of the arrowheads. As on the drawing of the cam-operated toy, a title block should be included to provide other necessary information.

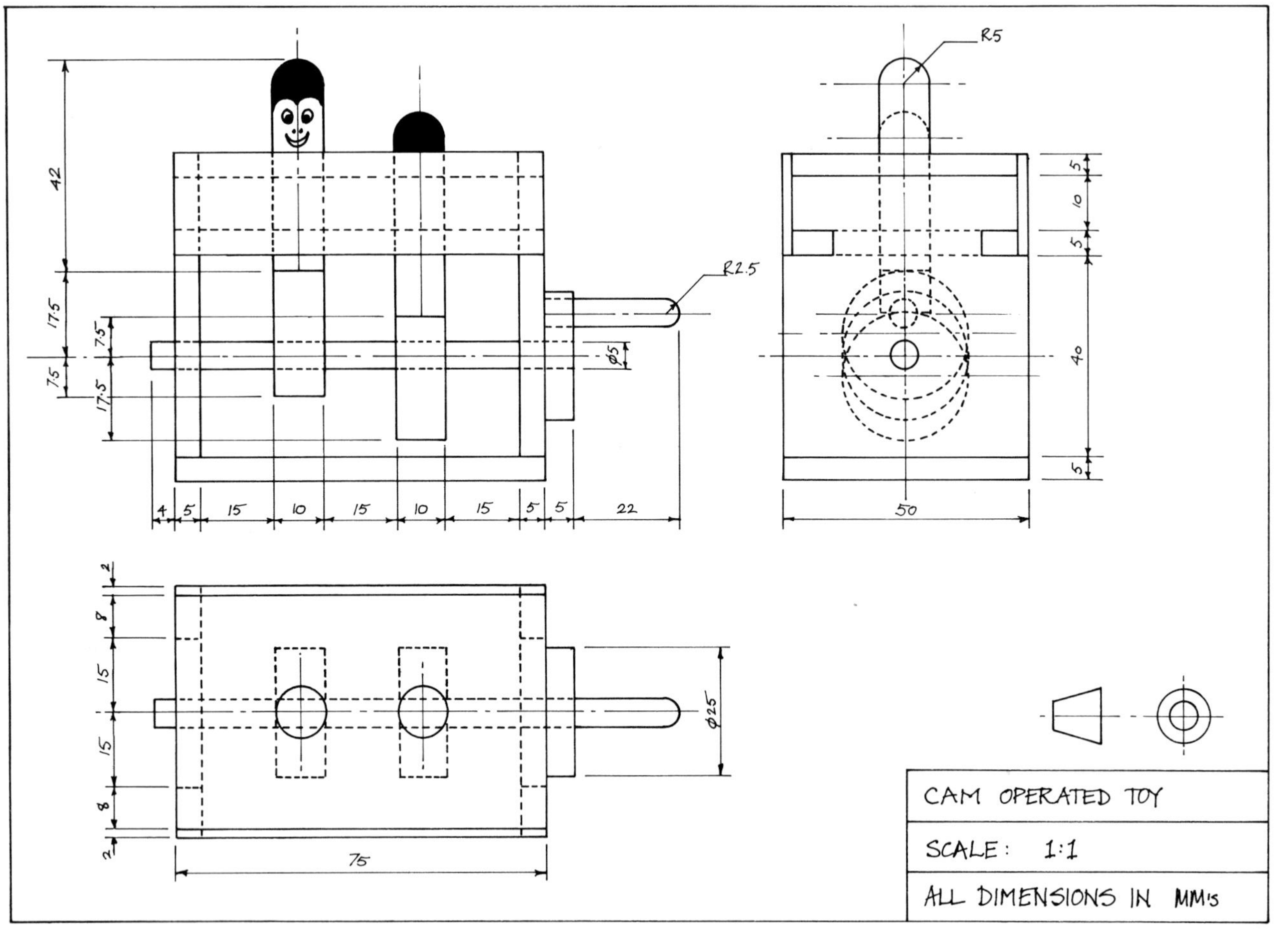

▸ THIRD ANGLE PROJECTION

In third angle projection, the positions of the elevations are different. Look back to page 23 to refresh your memory.

***Assignment**: Using words and diagrams, work out step-by-step instructions for making drawings in third angle projection.*

Assignment: *Using a small selection of Lego bricks and wheels, make a simple but interesting construction and then make an orthographic sketch in first angle or third angle. Decide on the size and scale of your drawing and make a final, measured orthographic drawing, which includes dimensions and a title block.*

▸ SECTIONS

A **sectional view** of an object shows what the object would look like if it was cut across. Sectional views are therefore sometimes called **cross-sections**.

Cross-hatched lines at 45° are used to show the areas that have been cut across, and different parts are cross-hatched using different spacings of line to distinguish them.

Colour can also be used (see page 47).

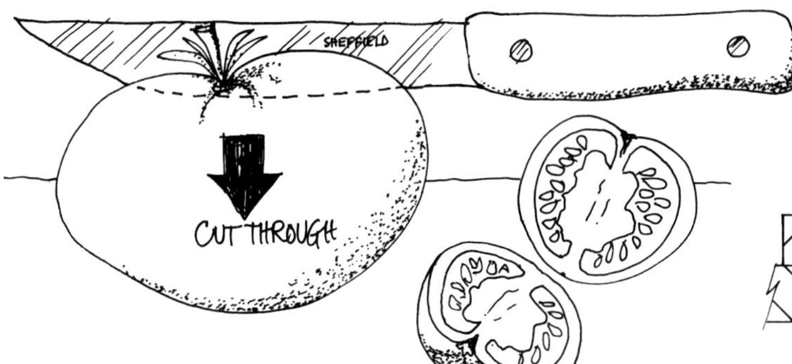

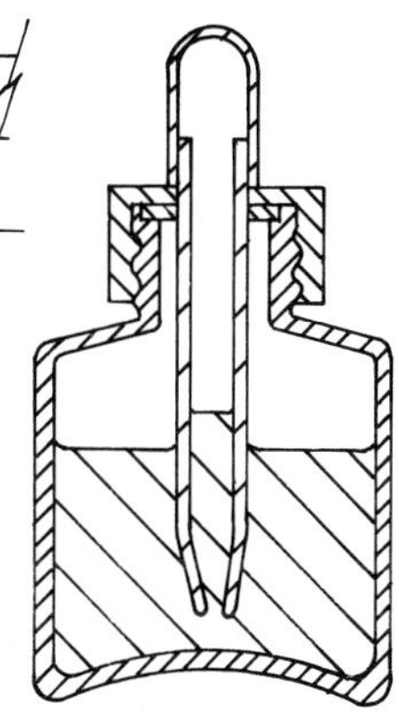

Cross sections of fruit and vegetables can be very good starting points for developing pattern designs using the window technique

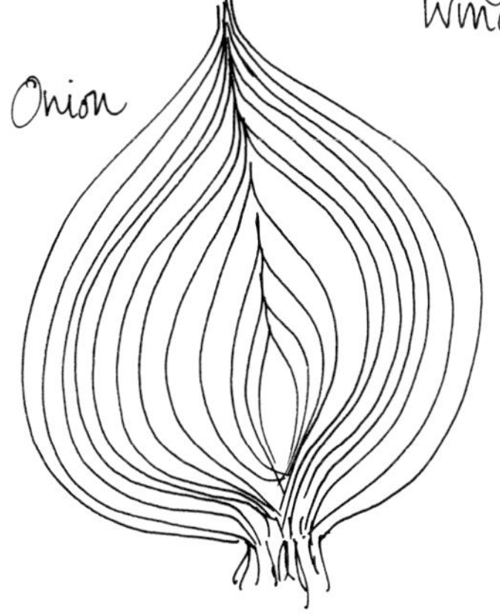

Assignment: *Make an orthographic drawing of a pencil sharpener five times full size. Include a sectional side elevation. Work out all the necessary details and measurements in rough first. Use your first drawing as an underlay and make another drawing using coloured areas instead of cross-hatching.*

AXONOMETRIC PROJECTION

Axonometric projection can be useful because it allows you to produce a three-dimensional view of an object using instruments where all the measurements, including circles, are *true*. It does, however, produce a distorted view because it does not allow for foreshortening.

To make an axonometric drawing, you will need a 45° set square. Start by drawing a **plan view** of the object at 45° to a base line. Next, project all the vertical lines upwards and then complete the form with lines at 45°. All circular objects can be drawn with compasses.

This method of drawing is sometimes called a **planometric** method, and it is used a lot by architects to create three-dimensional views from their plans.

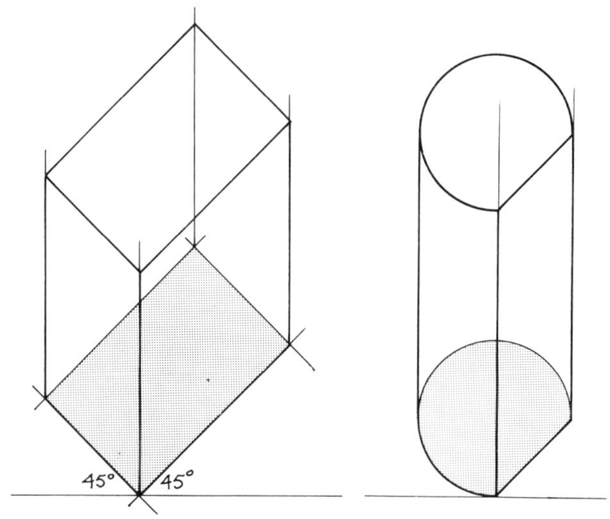

Axonometric projection can be very useful for producing exploded drawings. A centre line can be used to ensure that the separate parts of the object are positioned accurately.

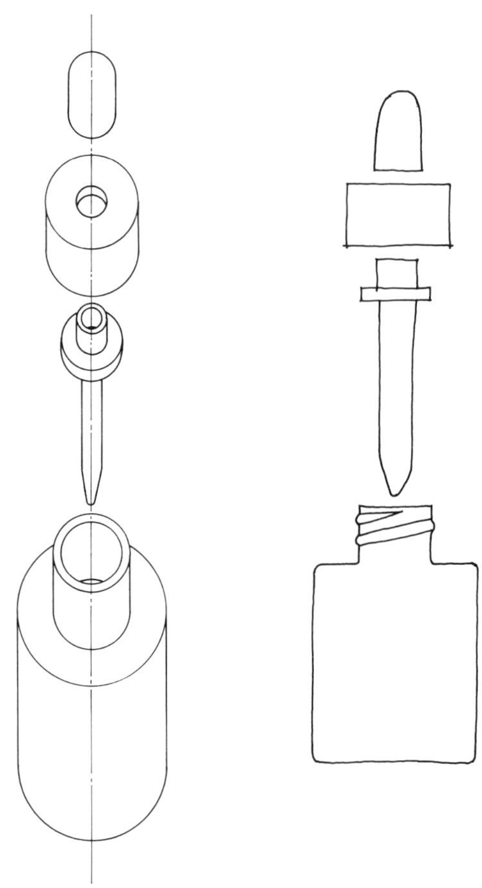

Assignment: *Make an axonometric projection from the orthographic drawing of your Lego construction (page 83).*

Presentation and mounting

The way you present finished work is most important. Good presentation will enhance your work; poor presentation will detract from it.

Always keep *all* your drawings, even your initial rough sketches. Number and date them so that you can keep them in order. At the end of a specific assignment, you may wish to present the work in a folder or binder. There are many types of binder available. Only use loose leaf ring binders, which require you to punch holes in your work, as a last resort. The best kind to use is the plastic spine type. In these, the spine is simply slid along the edge of the work to hold it together—no holes are necessary.

You should think about the cover of the folder carefully. One simple drawing or photograph together with careful lettering is usually adequate. The position of the information on the cover is also very important. Always position it towards the right-hand edge of the cover and line-up visuals and lettering accurately.

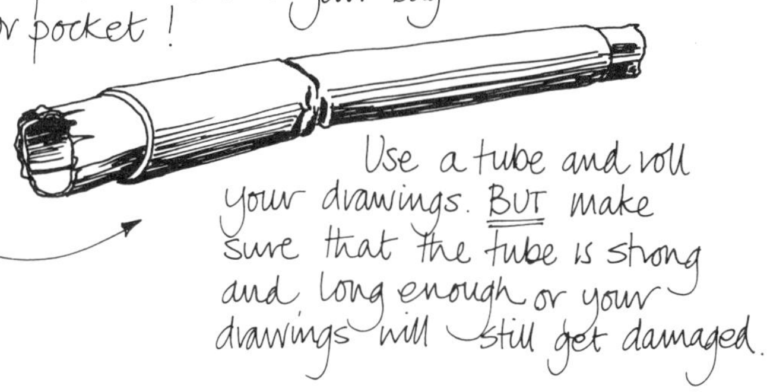

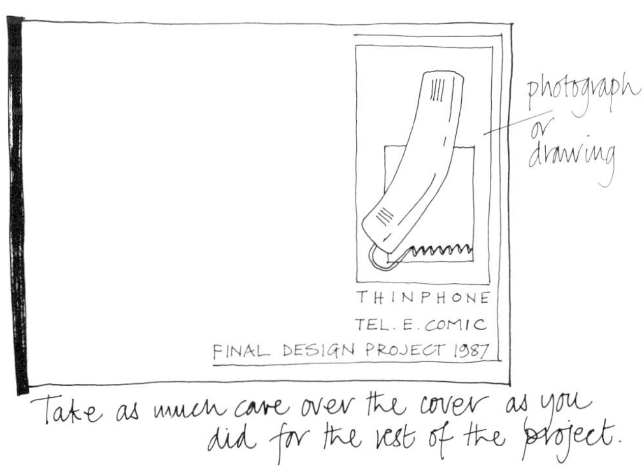

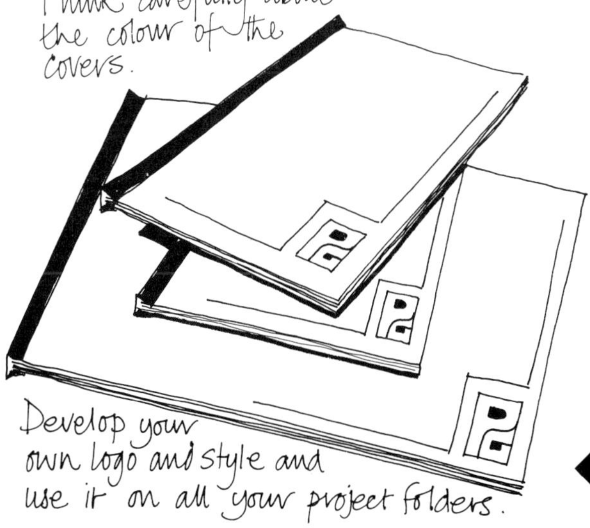

▸ MOUNTING DRAWINGS

Think about the placing of your work on the mounting surface. Random mounting will not enhance your work.

The colour of the mounting surface should be carefully considered. Neutral or pastel shades usually give the best effect.

Finished work can be mounted in one of two ways:

Surface mounting is where the finished work is fixed to the surface of the mounting sheet by means of adhesive such as Cow Gum, Spray-mount or Pritt. *Do not* use water-based liquid adhesives such as PVA, as these tend to distort the surfaces. Work can be mounted on sugar paper or card.

Window mounting is where a suitable-sized aperture is cut out of the mounting surface and the work positioned behind it using tape.

This method is more time consuming and involves accurate cutting with a craft knife. Window mounts can be made on paper, but mounting board gives a much more satisfactory finish.

Single drawings should be mounted with an equal border at the top and sides, but slightly wider at the bottom. This gives the feeling of a base to the mount.

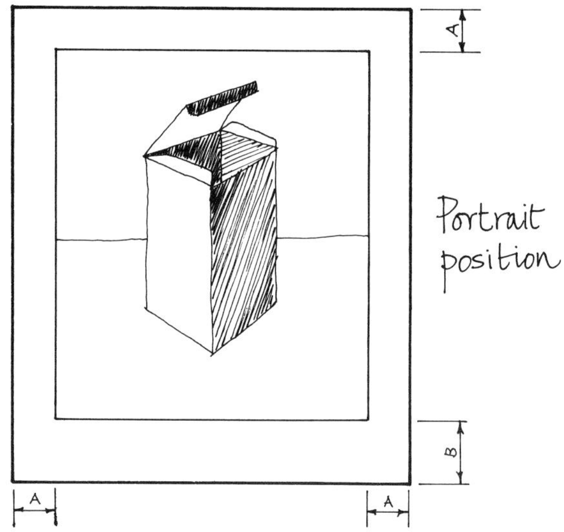

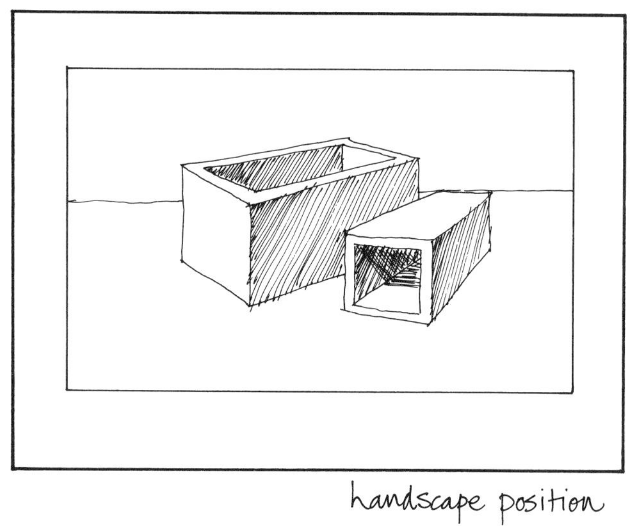

Multiple drawings can be mounted in three ways:

1. with the drawings forming a *border*, as in single mounting
2. with the drawings forming a *common central line*
3. Unusual-shaped drawings can be cut out and arranged to suit. Combinations of drawings and photographs can also be mounted in this way.

As a rule, try to mount the darkest and largest drawings at the bottom of the sheet. You can use both landscape and portrait positions for all methods.

Mounted with a common border

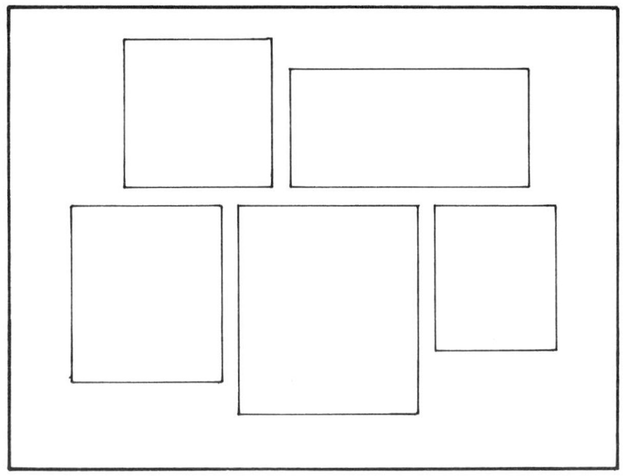

Mounted with a central line

▸ PHOTOGRAPHS

Mounting photographs carefully is important if they are to have the desired effect. Simply mounting whole photographs randomly or in rows can be very uninteresting. Quite often, the whole of the photo is not necessary. Don't be frightened to cut them and take away unwanted areas. However, it is best to keep one standard dimension, such as the height. The cut photos can then be mounted in a cartoon strip fashion, using an equal amount of space between each print.

Combination of orthographic and perspective views together with a photograph, help in the presentation of a place setter design for a disabled child. All three are window mounted

Window-mounted presentation renderings of a music console for a visually-handicapped and autistic child

Further assignments

Each of these assignments will require the use of a wide range of media if they are to be solved successfully. You will need to research, develop ideas through drawing and modelling, decide on a final design, then realize and evaluate it. In other words, you must follow a design cycle, as shown on page 5.

Assignment 1

You are a brilliant young designer setting up your own design agency. You need an interesting name and image which will attract attention and customers. Design a logo/symbol which can be used on all the agency's paperwork, such as notepaper, envelopes, design sheets, invoices, etc. Develop and model a three-dimensional version of the logo/symbol which can be given to customers at Christmas for use as a paper weight.

Think carefully about the following things:

- **a** *The kind of design work the agency is involved with.*
- **b** *A name for the agency. This may be affected by what the agency produces.*
- **c** *What kind of letter style will you use?*
- **d** *What colour/s will work best?*
- **e** *What size will the logo/symbol be in relation to notepaper, design sheets, etc?*

If you are stuck for ideas for names, look through Yellow Pages *or a design magazine.*

Assignment 2

Use the research you did on packaging (page 77) to help you answer this assignment.

Design and make a package for one of the following products:

- **a** *250 paper clips*
- **b** *100 smarties*
- **c** *5 floppy discs*
- **d** *a litre of milk*

Think carefully about the following things:

- **a** *the size and form of the package*
- **b** *the development of the package*
- **c** *a brand name for the contents*
- **d** *the visual appearance of the package, its colour, style of lettering, etc.*

Assignment 3

You have been engaged by a washing powder manufacturer to design a campaign to promote their new low-temperature biological washing powder. They require a leaflet that can be pushed through letter boxes, but it must be different from the usual type of handout. Design and make a leaflet which includes a humorous pop-up image which will promote this new product.

Think carefully about the following things:

- **a** *The initial impression of the leaflet. Many people throw this kind of material straight into the bin!*
- **b** *The humour must not offend potential customers.*
- **c** *The overall effect must be amusing so that the reader remembers the product.*

Assignment 4

You are unhappy with the present layout, furniture and decoration of your bedroom, and have been told by your parents that you can change them. Make a careful study of the room as it is, looking at the positions of light fittings, power points, furniture, etc.

Re-design the room. First, imagine you only had a limited supply of money, say £50. Then re-design the room again, this time assuming that money is no restriction. Make scale models of your solutions in an appropriate material.

Think carefully about the following things:

- **a** *What kind of atmosphere do you wish to create?*
- **b** *Will the answer to* **a** *affect your choice of colour and materials?*
- **c** *storage of books, records and tapes, clothes and shoes*
- **d** *a place to work*
- **e** *surfaces on which to put posters and photographs*
- **f** *If the room is small, how can you make it seem larger?*

For each of these assignments, you should produce a folder of work which shows evidence of research, sketches of your ideas, your final design, a production drawing and a model. You should also try to evaluate the final design to see if it completely answers the brief. Ask your friends what they think. Are there any ways in which the design can be improved?

Index